FRANCESCA SHAW

Keep It

*To anyone who still doesn't really know what you're doing with your life.
You will figure it out...eventually.*

And to my Mum, thank you for everything.

Contents

Content Warnings

This book includes mentions of sexual harassment and emotional abuse (off page, minor character only).

Playlist

'Better Man' *Paolo Nutini*
'Paris' *Taylor Swift*
'Halfway There' *Victor Ray*
'False Confidence' *Noah Kahan*
'Clean' *Noah Floersch*
'Lake Missoula' *Richy Mitch & The Coal Miners*
'On A Night Like This' *Niall Horan*
'Hot Mess' *Nick Rich*
'Babygirl' *Charlotte Clark*
'Beyond' *Leon Bridges*
'Hold It Down' *Noah Kahan*
'bad idea right?' *Olivia Rodrigo*
'People I Don't Like' *UPSAHL*
'Daydreams' *We Three*
'I Know Places' *Taylor Swift*
Bonus:
'Our Last Summer' *Mamma Mia Soundtrack*

Chapter 1

I gave myself one year. One year to 'make it' before I packed it in for good and got a job flogging insurance or office supplies or something in a depressing, solid nine to five. One year. That's it. Then obviously, one year turned into two and two into two and a half and so on and so forth until I ended up here, four years later a jack-of-all-trades at the bottom of the film industry ladder willing to be paid in meals and *experience*.

The film isn't a bad one. It's a surreal short about a woman who's being stalked by her past self and — yeah, okay it's not great. At least it's a job. A job in the middle of nowhere with fourteen hour days and a two-hour commute there and back. So what if I have to stuff extra bread rolls from the soup at lunch into my backpack so I can eat some form of dinner? It's experience. So what if I have to take a four hour round trip to pick up a smoke machine last minute and pay five hundred pounds out of pocket just to be told it's *no longer necessary?*

It's experience. Experience I need if I want to get anywhere close to fulfilling my dreams.

I just really didn't think the final tether holding my dream in my hand would be a power cord connected to a smoke machine.

"Yeah, we don't need that anymore. The director says it would make the scene look too cheap." The producer, Beth, tells me.

I really didn't think I'd give up on my dream on a foggy afternoon in Kent but standing in the middle of the forest with an apparently redundant smoke machine, is evidently enough to tip me over the edge.

A burst of laughter comes out of me. "You're joking."

In my university days, I would have held it together until I found my best friend Rosie on set and ranted to her about the audacity of sending me on a fool's errand in the middle of shooting. Rosie, of course, is nowhere near the outskirts of Kent since she had walked into a job in a post-production house the day after graduation. I wasn't jealous when Rosie was offered her job, we were going to be in different departments after all, but I couldn't help feeling bitter thinking about her glamorous city life working on the next wide-release feature while I've been stuck working for pennies on under-funded shorts.

"No," she says, turning her attention back to her iPad.

I close my eyes. After more late nights than I could count, over a hundred hours of driving and likely the same amount of pilfered bread rolls, I've had enough.

"That's it." I slam the smoke machine on the floor. "Fuck this. I'm out."

That makes Beth look up. "You what?"

"I quit. This is so not worth it. Find someone else to be your errand bitch. I'm basically a glorified delivery person."

Beth says nothing, her mouth slightly parted. "You can't quit, we haven't hired you."

I laugh, slightly manically. *"I know."*

I grab the smoke machine from the ground and walk away, finally feeling a weight fall off my shoulders. I'm going to go home, order a takeaway, drink a whole bottle of wine and watch a property development show.

"Wait!" I hear Beth shout from behind me. I don't stop.

* * *

"Do you know anyone in the market for a smoke machine?" I ask Rosie, holding my phone between my cheek and shoulder as I unceremoniously throw the forsaken thing on my passenger seat and start the engine.

"Why are you selling a smoke machine?" Rosie laughs.

"I've rented it for three days and I am not driving back to fucking Slough anytime soon." I sigh as I put my foot down, my little car already spluttering from the miles I've already put it through today.

"Okay, I feel like I am missing some very important pieces of information here."

I fill her in on my day from hell, gripping the wheel with both hands and trying to concentrate on the drive.

"You need to stop settling for crummy experience jobs, Annie," Rosie says after I finish my story, using the nickname she gave me in our first week as housemates in first year. "You need to aim higher."

"I am aiming higher," I protest. "It's just no one higher wants me."

"No, we are not having any of that self-pitying bullshit today, missy." Rosie scolds.

I groan and rest my palm on my forehead. "I can't *not* drown in self pity at the moment. I feel like everyone is already where they need to be and I am still basically at the same point in my career as I was when I was nineteen. I think I need to get used to the fact that I peaked in uni and pack it in."

Rosie sighs."Have you started drinking already?"

"I wish."

Rosie laughs. "Okay, first of all, don't give up yet. One shitty job—"

"Many shitty jobs. In a row!"

"Okay, fine, many shitty jobs do not mean you are a shitty filmmaker. Besides, you want to direct your own. Why don't you make your own film?"

I pout. That is a solution I had been playing with for months but I'd been making people's low-budget, non commissioned shorts for years now and they're always terrible. I want to direct my own film, sure, but I'd want to at least be commissioned for a mid-budget feature and not a kickstarted short. I can't get commissioned without at least having my name on a successful production and I can't get on a successful production without already being on a successful production. Besides, there was the stubborn voice in the back of my head that liked to question whether I even really wanted to direct anymore, but I wrote that off as insecurity and stamped down on it whenever it cropped up.

"I just—ugh, just let me moan for a bit before I start thinking about all of that. I've mainly got to figure out how my landlord will accept the bread rolls I've been paid in as rent. I'm going to be out by next week."

Rosie laughs. "Okay, why don't you come stay with me for a

bit, just to get you on your feet. You can sleep on the couch and earn some money in the pub over the road and then reassess whether you want to pack it in and go home."

"Would you actually?" I ask quietly.

"Babe, I've been dying for you to come crash here since I moved in," Rosie says.

"You're so good to me you know that?"

"I know, I get funding from the government for supporting the sad and unemployed."

After we hang up and my breakdown starts to progress into a slightly throbbing headache, I feel a little bit lighter. I might not have solved all of my issues tonight but at least I have a semi-plan. And that nagging voice in the back of my head can shut up.

* * *

Three weeks later I'm all moved into Rosie's London flat. And by moved in, I mean my two suitcases are open at the end of the bed and I spend my time rummaging for clean underwear. Rosie has even managed to get me a few shifts at The Old Crown working behind the bar for a cheery old man named Steve. It's not the nine-five routine I imagined as my backup but at least the money lining my bank account is relatively steady. Plus, it's better than standing outside in the freezing cold with a smoke machine (which I returned…eventually).

I still feel that nag of something — definitely *not* jealousy — when I see Rosie leave in the morning in her stylish work wear on her way to her cushy production house in Soho, but

I'm making money and getting back on my feet.

On one of my only Friday nights off, I'm waiting for Rosie to come home so I can open the bottle of vodka in my suitcase without feeling extremely alcoholic. Checking my phone for an update on my temporary roommate's ETA, I glance at the exchange we shared earlier.

Rosie: Send me your CV

Me: Why

Rosie: Send it and I'll tell you why

Me: CV.dox

Me: Why do you need my cv

Me: Why

Me: Rosie

Me: Why

Using my closed laptop as a table, I paint my nails whilst watching a rerun of the *Robin Carlson Show*. Jackson Harper is on making everyone laugh on the press tour for the new action blockbuster *Starboard Bound*, a film about the hijacking of a big boat, or cruise ship or whatever. He's joined by his co star Danny Covington who sits sulkily lapping up Harper's jokes and barely answering questions with more than two words. *Spoilsport*, I think bitterly.

"Honey, I'm home." Rosie shouts from the door as she kicks it shut behind her. "I brought food. Don't tell Steve because I got it from the Chinese place down the road and I don't want him to hate me."

I stand with a mock gasp and move into the kitchen, "Not the Golden Dragon, Rose. They've been competing for months. The amount of fliers I've already had to hand out over there is going to give me carpal-tunnel."

"Well, we'll hide the packaging so he will never need to

know," Rosie says, pulling out boxes of noodles.

"What's the occasion, anyway? You never order in." Unlike me, Rosie is a healthy person and believes having more than one meal a day of entirely processed and salted foods is bad for you.

"We're celebrating," Rosie says promptly.

I crunch my brow as I shovel egg fried rice into my mouth directly from the container. "Wha arr ee selebrashing?"

Rosie dishes up her food and grabs a wine bottle from the rack before we head back to the couch.

I wait for Rosie to tell me what we are celebrating, but instead she pours two glasses of wine. She hands one to me with one hand and snatches my plate away with the other, gently placing it on the coffee table as I'm still trying to stab a piece of broccoli with my fork.

"Oh my god, why bring food if you won't let me eat it?" I ask.

"*Because*," says Rose, "I am trying to tell you why we're celebrating."

"Okay, hit me."

"Our house just finalized a deal with Gwendoline Marcs."

Gwendoline Marcs is an up-and-coming director. They say up-and-coming but she has already had a few nods for her last and first feature *And Then They Met* and there are rumors she has another project lined up. She started directing when she was younger than me and now in only her mid-thirties, she's basically established herself as the next Scorsese in the making. I am, reasonably, obsessed with her.

"Oh my god Rose." I hug her. "That is so cool"

She grins. "I know we are all so buzzed. Grant brought us a round of drinks at lunchtime to celebrate. But that's not why we are excited tonight."

"What could possibly be more exciting than you working with Gwendoline Marcs?"

Her grin grows. "*You* working with Gwendoline Marcs."

I laugh. "As if."

"I am deadly serious."

The look in her eyes makes the laughter on my lips fade. "Wait— huh?"

Rosie tries to smother the grin on face, but her sparkling eyes give her away. "I don't know too much about the film yet, today was just an excuse for a piss-up. But basically from what I can tell it's being filmed exclusively in France and the main actor is a complete nightmare. It's all under NDA so no juicy details —although I bet they're a real diva."

I wait for Rosie to take a swig of her wine, vibrating with apprehension.

"*Anyway*," she continues, "apparently they're looking for a PA/assistant/runner person."

I gasp, "I'm a PA/assistant/runner person."

"I know," Rosie cackles. "So I was like, 'that's crazy my best friend is currently looking right now.'"

I am on top of the world.

"But they said no."

I fall, pitifully, back to earth.

"But *then* they said that they needed a French speaker."

And I'm up again. "I speak French!"

"I know!" Rosie laughs. "I told them you are fluent and half French and have a French passport and everything and guess what?"

"What?" I ask breathlessly, already knowing my best friend is going to pull through for me.

"They wanted to see your CV."

"*Shut the fuck up.*" I jump to my feet "Where's my CV?"

Rosie laughs, "You literally sent it to me earlier."

"You didn't tell me it was for Gwendoline Marcs, I didn't even double check it!"

"I looked at it before I sent it. Relax."

I place my hands over my pounding heart. "You did not do this for me."

"Of course I did this for you, have you met me? I'm amazing."

I laugh, "You are. If you get this for me I will marry you so you can have your EU passport."

"You were already going to do that, I was just waiting for the ring."

I laugh but say quietly. "This is—this is a lot right now."

I can feel Rosie smirking but don't look at her, instead I put my wine glass down and cover my face with my hands.

"I don't know if I can do it."

Thwack.

"What was that for?" I raise my hands against another pillow onslaught.

"Of course you can do it, you muppet! You're on the ball, you're great with cast *and* crew and *you speak French*. If you waste this opportunity because you're scared I will never speak to you again."

I groan. "But what about my job with Ste—"

Thwack.

"If you dare consider turning this down for that goddamn takeaway shop downstairs I will murder you in your sleep," Rosie hisses between hits.

"Fine! Would you—*ow*—would you stop that? It's just — whew, you know?" I breathe.

Rose exhales and loops her arm around my shoulders. "Okay, take a deep breath. I think this is your shot. You've got this Annie, I can feel it. This is gonna be it for you."

I close my eyes and breathe in deeply. I can imagine myself on set with a headset and clipboard, shouting at people to get to where Gwendoline Marcs needs them to be. I'll bring her coffee and she'll say, *'thanks Anya, good job'* and then she'll take me under her wing, mentor me until she eventually says in her Oscar's acceptance speech "I wouldn't be here today without the support of Anya Bonnet".

"Yes. Okay, yes, you're right. This is my shot."

Chapter 2

DANNY

I knew it was going to be an interesting day when I was pulled into a glass conference room for a meeting with my father. I could hardly remember the last time I have spent time with my family without the polished glare of a conference table between us. Even meetings with my sister happen across a table, albeit at a restaurant over a bottle of wine.

Swinging in my office chair to look out the tall glass window, I watch the workers outside with my chin in my hand. The professionals heading out on their lunch breaks with their blue suits and lanyards swinging from their necks. I've never had a lanyard and wonder idly if I could use one, even if just for my house keys.

The door opens and my father walks in. Charles Covington is an imposing man, his deep set frown lines marring the face so similar to mine. Charles raises his eyebrows and drops a script on the table with a thud, the paper sliding across the glossy surface.

I cough a laugh, my hand covering my burgeoning grin. I learned a long time ago to find humor in everything my father did. Not only does it infuriate Charles Covington but it makes the tension that fills my body fizzle away a little. I reach forward and grab the script.

Resting my ankle on my knee and flicking through the pages, I wait for my father to break the silence. I will read this script cover to cover just to avoid speaking to the man.

"You leave for Paris next week." The deep American voice drawls from the other side of the table. Charles has never lost his American twinge, even after all the years spent in London with my English-rose mother. I tried hard to cling to the home counties accent I developed at school, refusing to be associated any more with the man who raised me than I have to.

"No audition?" I ask mildly.

"Don't be smart, Daniel," Charles clutches the chair in front of him. I haven't auditioned since *Better You Know.* "It's with Gwendoline Marcs and it's a summer shoot. On location in Paris. You can't fuck it up."

I run my fingers through my hair, "Do I even get a say?"

Redness starts spreading up my father's throat, his tell that he's about to explode. "No, you don't get a say. Do you know how many strings I pulled to get you this gig?"

I'm sure the *strings* he pulled were sending a single email. Pip has already told me that Charles was producing a new feature. Pip always gets the news before I do.

"What if I don't want to do it?"

"I don't give a fuck if you don't want to do it, your contract is signed."

"Hmm, I don't remember signing anything." It's truly second nature to be as ornery as possible with my father.

"You will do this job, Daniel. You will behave perfectly, you will do a good job, you will promote the shit out of this film and you will be goddamn happy about it."

"I'm not listening to this." I stand up, throwing the script back on the table. I move to push past my father but he blocks my way.

"You will listen and you will do this," my father's beady eyes glare.

I clench my jaw and take a seat, my blood boiling.

"You'll have top billing."

As if that's an enticement.

"What's it about?" I ask, leafing through.

"Do I look like Wikipedia? Read it yourself for Christ's sake. I'm sure you remember how to."

I flick through the script. Conveniently, what are evidently my lines have already been highlighted, most likely thanks to my father's PA Georgia. Of course, I won't even be allowed the dignity of going through my own script.

I worked with an actor years ago who combed meticulously through every page, considering every word and inflection. I watched her study her book like she was preparing for an exam, and I couldn't help but credit it with her enviable performance. I had wanted to learn from her, and really pay attention to the words coming out of my mouth, not just memorize like a robot. The next time my father handed me a project, I had asked for a clean script. He didn't even reply.

The script in my hands feels heavy, thick, long. Picking out lines at random, I have a small tickle in the back of my brain that this job might be different from the other superficial projects I've had before. Closing the book and placing it back on the table, I turn my attention back to my father.

Before I can open my mouth my father opens his. "We're hiring you a personal for this one."

"Eric?" I say, referring to the PA I have used before. I like Eric because he was more like a chill cousin than an employee, he never pressured me to do anything I didn't want to do and mostly just left me alone.

Charles guffaws. "Not a chance, you'll get a PA through production."

I glare at my father.

"And before you complain, I don't have anything to do with it," he says, throwing his hands up in mock surrender. "That's all. You'll get the train on Sunday, Georgia will send you an email."

"The train?" I ask.

"Production is focusing on its carbon footprint." Charles stands, pushing his chair back under the desk. "I'll fly out in the first few weeks to see how you're getting on." *To make sure you stay out of trouble.*

Charles turns and pulls the door open. "Don't fuck this up and don't embarrass me, Daniel." He doesn't even look at me as he strides from the room.

I lean back in my chair, content to wait for my father to be well out of the vicinity. Heaven forbid I get stuck in the elevator with the man.

Stuffing the script in my bag, I run my hands through my hair and take a breath. *It's one more job,* I tell myself, *one more.*

Slinging my bag over my shoulder, I stomp to the elevator. My hand itches in my pocket on the long descent to street level.

Stepping out into the fresh spring air, I pull my vape out of my pocket and take a drag of the cherry flavor. I switched from cigarettes after some nagging from Pip. I had rolled my eyes when I first started to find the little pink sticks in my empty cigarette cartons but I appreciated what my sister was trying to do. It's taken years to have anything resembling a close relationship with my sister, so now I'll do anything to make her happy. Even if it means using the poor substitute for the real thing.

Pulling my headphones in and blasting a rock song, I shoulder my way down the street. I take a deep breath and watch my feet, glancing up under my lashes at everyone who passes me by. The tension in my shoulders aches, and I know I will have to lock the door twice behind me when I get home just to feel secure.

Checking the time I decide it's early enough to get the tube home without any issue. My father pays for a car service, but my reluctance to use his money sometimes overtakes my need for privacy — today being one of those days.

The tube carriage isn't crowded but I stand near the door, facing away from the rest of the carriage. I learned a few years ago that this was the best way to remain inconspicuous.

I finally take my first easy breath when my front door slams behind me. I dump my bag on the floor and flop onto the couch. The ticking of my watch echoing through the empty room like a metronome. Opening my eyes I glance at my bag, the corner of the manuscript poking out.

I pull it out and settle into the couch.

One more job, I tell myself, *one more.*

Chapter 3

ANYA

By the time Monday morning rolls around I'm running on four packets of biscuits and nerves. Rosie is absolutely no help whatsoever. Saying *'You'll be fine'* and *'Stop getting crumbs in my duvet'* when I huddle in my temporary bed with a packet of cookies contemplating the best way to answer the phone; 'Hi' is too casual and 'Good Afternoon, you have reached Anya Bonnet' too formal.

I call into work claiming the flu so that I can have the whole day to panic but it's not until four pm that my phone lights up with a call.

I freeze and stare at the screen for a split second before picking it up so quickly that it nearly flies out of my grasp.

I clear my throat as I press answer.

"Hello, Anya speaking." I cringe.

"Hello, this is Devon from *Accordance*. We are looking at you for a PA position. I have it here that you studied for three years at the University of Thornton with a first in Film/TV Production – is that correct?"

"I—yes—"

"And you have had experience on multiple short films on

the festival circuit but nothing mainstream or commercial?"

"Well no but—"

"And you have directed two short films, one going on to win three times at local film festivals?"

I'm quite proud of that one. "Yes."

"And you speak fluent French?"

"Oui," I reply with a jaunty tone.

"Do you have a French passport?"

"Yes."

"And do you have a base in Paris?"

"Uh—" I stumble. My aunt has a place in the sixteenth arrondissement but I haven't spoken to her in years. I don't even know if she still lives there. I can hear the silence stretching down the phone and my opportunity running away with it. "Yeah, yeah, I have a base."

"Okay, we will need to do some more checks but that all sounds great. We will contact you in a few days with the contract details."

Wait, what?

"Wait, what?" I ask, incredulously. "Are you saying I have the job?"

"Well yes, this all seems in order. Do you have any questions?"

My mind goes blank. I know I had questions but what were they? "So I have the job? Just like that?"

"Yes," Devon says, "The contract and details for your role will be sent to you by the end of the week."

"Uh—th—thank you!"

"Goodbye."

What. The. Actual. Fuck. Did I just get a job on a Gwendoline Marcs feature film in a five-minute phone call? I check the time on my screen – scratch that three minutes and twelve seconds. My stomach soars and I laugh incredulously.

I sent a text to Rosie full of exclamation marks and ring my mum immediately.

"*Salut, mon petit cabbage.*" Mum chirps down the phone.

"Mum I got the job!" I screech.

"What job?" Mum exclaims, matching my energy even without any information.

"A job on a Gwendoline Marcs feature!"

"Gwendoline Marcs! Wow!"

I laugh, "You don't know who that is do you?"

"Well no, but you do." Mum says. "Go on, tell me every-thing."

I stumble over my words telling the whole story from the demented smoke machine to Rosie's text to the call with Devon. Mum interrupts with the appropriate exclamations.

"So when do you start?"

"I don't know yet, I'll get the contract in soon."

"I'm so proud of you, cabbage." Mum had been calling me cabbage ever since I was a child. She used to say the French term of endearment until I was old enough to know what it meant. I used to be so cross that my mum was calling me a root vegetable that Sabine Bonnet started to just call me Cabbage just to wind me up. And it stuck.

"Uh, there is one thing." I play with the end of my hair.

"What?"

"I told them I have a base in Paris."

Silence.

"Why did you say that?"

"I don't know! I panicked." I pull at my lip tentatively. "Do you think Aunt Claudette will let me stay at hers?"

I hear mum's sigh down the phone.

"Please?" I ask. My mother and her sister do not have an easy relationship. I've never really known why they don't get on but I always know to approach the subject gently.

"Mum," I say quietly.

"I'll text her," she huffs. "But if she says no then you're going to have to start searching."

I pump my fist. "Thankyouthankyouthankyou."

Later, after I've been to visit Steve and put in my notice, I'm opening a bottle of supermarket prosecco when a text comes through from mum.

Mum: Claudette is 'summering' in the Alps so her apartment is all yours.

The bottle pops and I feel like an Formula 1 driver, basking in my victory.

Chapter 4

ANYA

The email with my contract comes through the Friday after the call and by Saturday morning, I have my Eurostar ticket in my inbox.

Pulling my suitcase down the aisle of the train, I glance up at the seat numbers overhead. I've never sat in Business class before. The aisle is significantly bigger with two seats on one side of the aisle and one on the other. Hopefully, I can sit on my own and not have to worry about awkwardly brushing elbows with a stranger.

My suitcase snags on the corner of a seat and I tug it impatiently. I am already overheating in my coat and I can feel sweat slide down my back.

Finally, I spot C24. Double checking my ticket I realize with a twinge of annoyance that my seat is indeed a two and to make it worse there is already a man sitting next to it. I was hoping for the window at least but if production is paying then I'm not complaining.

The man hasn't looked up at me yet but I can see the mess of brown curls on his head and the long slender fingers holding his phone.

I place my case in the overhead container and settle in my seat, grabbing my own phone from my pocket. The motion of my arm bending finally causes C25 to look up.

I feel his stare on me, burning the side of my face.

"What are you doing?" the stranger asks. His brown hair falls haphazardly across his forehead as if he has run his hands through it, familiar blue eyes glare at me from beneath–frankly ridiculously–long eyelashes.

Stunned, I glance into the aisle, looking for whoever he must be talking to before turning back to him. "Excuse me?"

"What are you doing?" he repeats, as if the question suddenly makes sense.

"Sitting in my seat." I try not to phrase it as a question.

He blinks. "Sit somewhere else."

"What? No. This is the seat on my ticket."

"Let me see it."

"See what?"

"Your ticket." He reaches out a hand, his fingers curling impatiently as if he expects me to hand it over.

"My tick–God, Eurostar are a lot more casual with the uniforms nowadays."

The daggers C25 shoots me are so icy I could get freezer burn, but I meet him with a glare of my own.

"This isn't your seat."

I stamp down on the nervousness that maybe I am in the wrong seat. I remind myself I've already read my ticket and to refuse to give this guy an inch by checking again.

"Yes, it is."

"No, it's not."

Unbelievable. "If you want to move, be my guest." I bite out.

His nostrils flare. A shame, for it convolutes his strong

Roman nose into a ghastly sneer.

"I was here first."

"Well, if you're not going to move and you can't make *me*, you're just going to have to get over it." I send him a saccharine smile and turn back to face the front.

1 - 0 C25.

In an attempt to make myself even more at home, I start to shed my layers.

Spring is well under way in England but the weather has never abided by the calendar, and it's been unseasonably cold. Which is why I am wearing a t-shirt, jumper, coat and a fetching lilac bobble hat. I can see now that it might have been overkill, as the run to the train–and the infuriating fight with Grumpy–has left me slightly overheated.

Praying I don't smell and can avoid any further vitriol from C25, I aggressively strip layers, leaving them in a pile in my lap.

"It's May." The dry voice pipes up.

I groan, glaring at the seat in front of me. "Barely. And I run cold." I pull off my hat.

Finally, the announcement of departure blares over the speaker and the train begins to pull away from the station.

I pull a tattered paperback out of my backpack and settle in, I only peek at C25 once and see him leaning back with his eyes closed. His moodiness at my *sitting in a seat* has momentarily ceased, and my eyes linger on his face. His long lashes brush against smooth cheekbones and a strong jaw. When he's not sneering, C25 is actually rather handsome, I guess, although his personality has made that dry up like a good tea towel.

The train speeds through the countryside and from previous trips, I know the tunnel is coming up. I turn my attention to the window, pointedly not looking at the man sitting in front of it.

"Although you might believe it, you can't actually see any fish through the tunnel." C25 perks up sarcastically. He's watching me through the glass reflection.

"I know that," I say with as much venom as I can – despite the fact that I definitely did think you could see into the ocean when crossing the tunnel connecting the UK to mainland Europe, and had thought that until I was well into my teens.

I don't know what it is about this stranger that makes me want to be as childish as possible, but I've ridden the wave too long to stop now.

He raises a brow, his mouth twitching.

We emerge from the tunnel and the countryside outside the window passes in a blur that I watch out of the corner of my eye, refusing to acknowledge the man beside me. Pulling out my phone, I scroll through my emails, intending to get ahead of my first day tomorrow. I try to refresh, in case someone has sent me fresh instructions or the call sheet has come through but the signal is sluggish.

Huffing, I reach into my bag for my charger. The socket is underneath the seat so I reach between me and the stranger. Unable to see, I fold myself in half, fiddling until I can get the wire plugged in. The man's denim clad leg shifts uncomfortably. Straightening up and barely able to avoid hitting my head on the seat in front, I settle.

"Are you done?"

"Yes," I reply in a prim voice.

The man shifts some more and clears his throat. "Can I borrow your charger?"

I raise my eyebrows, "Excuse me?"

He shakes his phone in front of my face. "My phone's dead."

"You didn't bring your own charger?" I ask incredulously. "To a different country?"

"I forgot it," he bristles.

"Not my problem." I reply, folding my phone underneath my arms protectively. The audacity of this man.

He blinks at me as if he's never been refused such a request before. "Come on, you're on like seventy percent."

"Still have thirty percent to go."

He huffs and slumps in his seat, his head resting on the window like a petulant child.

I cross my arms over my chest and tuck my phone between them securely. I lean my head against the seat and attempt to get some sleep.

I blink awake some time later. From the corner of my eye, I see he is still slumped against the window, his eyelashes dusting his cheekbones. Glancing at my phone and it's full battery, I spot his sitting on the tray table. Deciding to be the bigger person, I quickly unplug my phone and put his on charge. I glance at him to ensure he is really asleep. He doesn't move but I swear I see his lips twitch.

The announcement rings that we are arriving soon, and the man wakes up. He starts using his phone, not acknowledging the charger that has suddenly appeared.

As we pull into the station, I glare at the phone in his hand still plugged into the seat beneath us. I try to catch his eye but he is steadfastly ignoring me. No 'thank you' incoming, then.

Huffing slightly, I grab his hand, the cool metal of the sleek phone in sharp contrast to the warm skin of his knuckles. I ignore the tingle that sparks at my fingers. I avoid his smirk as he turns his body towards me and the feel of his large, warm hand still under mine. Without looking at him, I tug my charger until it's free from his phone. I sit up, fighting back my blush. I just manhandled a complete stranger. I think I might have left my common sense on the other side of the tunnel.

At least when I get off this train, I won't ever have to see him again.

I get up to pull my bag from the overhead, but before I can, C25 stands in a fluid motion. His arms lift, his muscles bunching under his sweater as he grabs my bag and drags it down, handing it to me. My pulse races at the movement, who does that? Who is this man who is so rude one minute and almost swoon-worthy the next?

"Thanks," I mumble, pushing my hair behind my ear.

"Thanks for the charger," he replies.

I nod and shuffle into the aisle, swallowed up in the orderly queue of people. Glad to be rid of him.

As soon as I disembark, my phone rings. I pull my suitcase to a stop and answer.

"Ah Anya, finally got through."

"Devon," I straighten, coming to a halt on the platform, "Sorry, I was on the train and had no signal."

"It's fine, you were busy." Devon brushes it off.

My senses twitch but I ignore them. Yes, busy being locked in a battle of wills with my seatmate.

"Anyway," Devon starts, "How was it?"

"Uhm," Is this how the industry is? Is everyone this polite about traveling? "Fine." Apart from the irritatingly attractive stranger.

"I know Danny can be difficult, typical really." Wait, *what*? "You know how these actors are."

My stomach drops. *Danny?*

"Uh—" I start.

"So Georgia has sent over the full job spec, this has come from the big boss obviously. It's pretty detailed, hotel, transport etcetera, but good to have as a reference." Growing dread climbs up my throat. "If you could make sure he gets to the hotel okay? He has the details too. And I'll see you tomorrow on set. He's coming in with the boss so don't worry tonight but from the end of play tomorrow you'll need to be stuck to him like glue, okay?"

"Like glue," I mutter, turning back to the train. The crowd of people disembarking flood around me as I stand frozen on the platform.

Devon hangs up with a "See you tomorrow".

I instantly open my email, and it doesn't take long for me to see the document it would have been helpful to receive four hours ago.

DANNY COVINGTON DETAILS.

Danny Covington.

Danny Covington, household name, nepotism baby, heart-throb, star of teen blockbuster *Better You Know*, main feature of the poster hanging above my bed from the ages thirteen to fifteen.

A throat clears and I lift my head. Danny Covington is standing right in front of me.

Those swimming blue eyes twinkle despite the cocky smirk twisting his soft lips.

"I've got it from here." he says, sardonically. "I'll see you tomorrow, freckles." He pulls a navy baseball cap out of his pocket and pulls it on his head. "Oh, and if you could get a charger sorted that would be great." He doesn't spare me a glance as he walks off into the crowd.

I watch his retreating figure in stunned silence. I'm in big trouble.

Chapter 5

ANYA

To make life just that little bit harder, the queue for the metro tickets stretches for miles. I do a quick glance around for Danny Covington but when I can't spot him, I assume he called a car. Which then makes me feel worse. Despite what Devon said on the phone, I know that a good first impression would have been to get the car sorted.

Of course a better first impression would have been to allow the man to charge his phone on the train. God, I'm such an idiot. How did I not even recognize him? I just thought he was a regular hot guy, it never crossed my mind that he was a famous movie star.

Tugging my suitcase onto the métro and squeezing into a seat, I'm confident I know where I'm going so I don't bother consulting a map. Which is obviously a mistake as I miss my change at Strasbourg-Saint Denis and have to spend an extra fifteen minutes going back on myself.

I refuse to pull my phone out of my pocket to check a map, determined not to read the rest of *that* email until I'm safely behind four walls and able to freak out in peace. Surely, I can't be expected to work closely with Danny Covington. I'm a *nobody*. Why would they trust *me* with one of the most famous men in the world?

When I finally emerge onto street level, I take a deep inhale, allowing my mind to take a breath. The area is quiet and residential, with a small cafe perched on the corner and a few boutiques dotted along the street. It has been a few years since mum and I have visited Paris but I can still remember sitting at a bistro table whilst my mum and Claudette devoured a bottle of rosé and I nursed an fizzy orange drink.

I turn a corner and wander down the street, the tip of the Eiffel Tower just visible over the top of the gray rooftops.

I finally pull my suitcase to a stop in front of the large burgundy door. Fishing my phone out of my pocket, I pull up the text from Claudette.

Claudette: Pin is 7825 and the key is under the mat on the fourth floor, I might pop in in a few months. Bisous x

Shouldering my backpack, I tap the pin into the keypad and open the door to the small marble lobby. Raising my eyebrows at the grandeur, I squeeze into the cramped elevator at the end of the hall.

The elevator doesn't have any numbers so I press what I hope is the fourth floor and wait for the rickety room to move. Disembarking, I wander down the short corridor until I find the first door with a doormat. None of the other doors offer one and I idly wonder if Claudette bought it just for the aesthetic of leaving a key underneath. Snatching the key from its hiding place I shoulder open the door.

Pulling it closed behind me, I take in what I instantly dub 'Chez Claudette'. The small entrance hall is clean and suave with parquet flooring and paneled walls, to the right is a small kitchen with cream cupboards and a large window over the sink. The next room is a medium sized bathroom with a shower. Turning to the left, I head through the double saloon doors and into a large living room complete with two Juliet balconies and a plush cream couch.

Taking my coat off, I pull my phone out of my pocket. Pushing my hair out of my face I press call.

"What's it like?" Mum asks as soon as she answers.

"Well," I reply, flipping the camera, "I feel like I'm in Architectural Digest."

Giving Sabine a quick tour interrupted with the occasional *'Ooohh'* from her, I explore my new home away from home. Pulling back the light curtains I look out onto the street, already bustling with traffic and people.

"This feels like an Airbnb, does she even live here?" I ask, taking in the curated furniture.

"Oh, who knows," Mum says. "Look in the wardrobes, what stuff does she have?"

I laugh, "I'm not going to snoop through her things," I open the bedroom wardrobe. "There's nothing here anyway. She must rent it out, surely."

"Maybe she doesn't even live in Paris and she just likes to rent out a random Airbnb and pretend that it is her home so she can show off for us." Mum muses.

I laugh, "I mean she's your sister so I guess it's possible."

"Very funny," Mum chastises, "Have you got any food in?"

I collapse on the comfortable couch, my energy depleted. "No. I'll head out now and see if I can get some stuff."

"How was the train?" I immediately curse the fact that I video called as it's impossible to hide the flicker of disdain that crosses my face. "What happened?" she asks knowingly.

"Nothing, I just had a rude man sitting next to me." I rub

my hand across the soft cushion under my arm.

"What! What did he do? Did you report him?" Sabine asks incredulously, already ready to fight.

"Calm down, he was just grumpy." I don't tell her that it turns out I will have to put up with him a lot more than just one train journey. "Look, I'm going to head out now, see if I can get some bread or something."

"Okay, petit chou, text me later, " Mum says, "and good luck for tomorrow." With a blown kiss through the camera, I hang up the phone. Staring around the apartment that I'm maybe a little bit convinced is a rental, I text my Aunt thank you for the place and take a deep breath.

Surely, my job isn't to babysit Danny Covington? Yes, I had signed the contract and NDA without really looking at it, but I was sure there wasn't a job description on there, only the financial bottom line.

Scrolling through my emails I pull up the one from Devon with the job offer.

"Fuck." I mutter.

Deciding not to think about it I check the time and decide it's still early enough to explore. Divesting myself of my layers, I pull a brush through my hair and add a swipe of lipstick before swanning out the door.

I don't really know what to do once I leave the apartment, wandering the streets until I find a supermarket that looks promising. I meander through the aisles, picking up a baguette, some cheese and a bottle of wine. I stop in the electrical aisle and quickly snatch a phone charger off the shelf. After I pay and place my items in my tote bag, my baguette peaking out the top, I feel positively local.

I don't think about Danny Covington, or about the job I'm

set to start tomorrow. I have my wine and my bread and a place to sleep. Tomorrow's problems can be battled tomorrow.

I eventually wander towards the Eiffel Tower, its imposing silhouette my constant companion on my flaneur. The Trocadero is packed with people taking photos, buskers and floggers selling their wares and couples making out. Sidestepping them I veer left and find a small secret park tucked away from the bustle. Using my coat as a blanket, I plop on the grass and pull my bread out of my bag. I'm tempted to grab the wine and just down the whole bottle but decide against descending into alcoholism this soon into my failed career. No, not failed. Yet. Taking a big bite of my baguette, I settle into my spot. Even if the job is a disaster, at least I'm doing something. Life could be a lot worse.

I stay in my little slice of heaven with my bread until the sun goes down.

Chapter 6

ANYA

The next morning, I'm a wreck. Sleep the night before was evasive, even in Claudette's luxurious bed with the sounds of the city seeping through the Juliet balcony. I have managed to look presentable; pulling on jeans and a t-shirt, swiping some mascara on my eyelashes and concealer on my dark circles.

Following the address on the call sheet, I catch the metro to the edge of the Bois de Boulogne. Production has commandeered an empty car park at the edge of the park, large white trailers propped haphazardly behind temporary gates.

Taking a deep breath, I head to what looks like the entrance. A beefy security guard steps into my path holding out a hand.

"*Désolé mademoiselle vous ne pouvez pas venir ici.*"

"*Oh, je travaille ici,*" I pull out my phone, unlocking the screen with sweaty fingers and showing him the call sheet.

The guard nods and lets me pass.

Glancing around the base, I take a shaky breath. What now? I stand, biting my lip until a blonde woman jumps out of a truck, radio stuck to the belt loop of her jeans.

Gathering my courage, I head in her direction.

"Uhm hi?" I say, embarrassment rising. "I'm Anya, I'm a

PA?"

The blonde woman blinks at me for a few seconds before saying "Production is that one." She points to the truck she emerged from.

I mutter a thank you as the woman darts off. I can't help but feel that I have already committed a grave faux pas but have no idea what it could have been. And it was probably not worse than the train journey from hell. Shaking off the memory, I head to the production truck.

After I lightly tap on the door, it swings open to reveal a brunette woman balancing on the top step, a pen resting behind her ear.

"Anya?" she asks.

"Yes, hi." I offer my hand.

The woman shakes my hand with a bemused smile. "Devon, Production Coordinator. We spoke on the phone. Come on in and meet everyone." She steps back to let me step into the trailer.

I have never been in an official film trailer before, this one is kitted out like a mini office on wheels. Wooden desks are stacked basically on top of each other and miles of papers are pinned to the walls.

Inside there are three desks littered with papers and empty coffee cups. An older man with blond thinning hair looks up from his laptop and gives me a half smile.

"This is Brian the Production Manager. This is Sarah our 2nd AD, and you've just missed Rachel our 1st." A woman with short brown hair pulled back in a slick bun gives me a friendly wave. "You'll meet our Line Producer David and Michael the Producer later, they're in a meeting with the Exec's at the minute."

"Hi," I say shyly.

"Well," Devon says. "Let me give you a quick tour." I spin around on my heels and jump back down the stairs. Devon follows and pulls the door behind her. "I don't usually give tours but I didn't want to say this in the truck. I'll be honest, I'm not really sure what your job is."

Thank god, I think. "Yeah, the job description I got was pretty vague." I force out a fake chuckle.

"Basically, from what I can tell — Danny is a bit…well… he's difficult apparently. And the producers figured having someone on his back 24/7 would be the best way to ensure he's…handled."

"Handled." I echo.

Devon nods as if I'm picking up what she's putting down. "Exactly."

"So…like his assistant?"

"Exactly," Devon repeats. "Well, I guess it could be described more as a babysitter."

At my raised eyebrows Devon rushes to reassure me. "Not that that's what you'll be doing. Anyway, you know what these actors are like, more like toddlers than anything else. They just need a bit of attention and a lot of wrangling."

I absorb this. A babysitter? For a grown man. "Isn't this the 2nds job?" I ask. On a set this size, the second assistant director would be in charge of the cast; getting them on set on time and catering to their various needs.

"Well, yes usually," Devon says. "But the boss decided Danny would need a personal. They were going to hire someone from their side, but Gwen put her foot down and fought for you."

I feel dizzy, *Gwendoline Marcs fought for me?* But I'm a

nobody. I find myself nodding.

"Is this making sense?" Devon asks before clicking her fingers. "Oh, and you speak French, yeah?"

"Yeah," I reply. "I mean *oui*."

Devon laughs, "Great, I think that's just a precaution but we don't have that many French speakers on set so it's always a good weapon in the arsenal. Right, I need to get back in there but we are going to need Danny in makeup in —" she checks her watch "—twenty five minutes. His trailer is the last one on the left, can't miss it. Let me know if you need anything." Devon calls over her shoulder.

I feel like I've been caught in a whirlwind. Gwendoline Marcs had fought for me? Or, at least, my job. And I haven't even considered seeing Danny again after the debacle from yesterday.

Not wanting to wait around like a spare part, I wander towards what I presume is the catering truck. I grab a cup and pour myself a coffee, praying I'm actually allowed to make it myself.

"Hi," a voice sounds at my side causing me to jump and nearly spill my drink. A girl, at least a few years younger than me with a long blonde braid resting over her shoulder, smiles at me shyly. "I'm Jess, the base runner. Devon sent me over to say hi. So hi." She chuckles nervously.

"Nice to meet you, I'm Anya." I hold my hand out for her to shake. "Have you been on this for long?"

"A few days, we're still setting things up so I've just been running around doing this and that. Mostly making sure we've got enough water, I never considered how many gallons of water would be needed to keep a set going, we've already gone through five bottles and we've only been here a few days.

"

I smile at her, unable to get a word in if I tried. I try to subtly return to making my drink, hoping I'm not coming off as rude.

"Sorry I'm rambling, I do that when I'm nervous," she blurts, barely stopping for breath. "It's my first time on a big set."

I grin at her and lean forwards conspiratorially. "Me too."

Her eyes bug, "Really? But you're working so close with Danny Covington."

"Don't remind me," I mutter, pouring an extra sugar into my coffee.

The radio at Jess's hip bleeps, and she presses her hand to her ear. "I need to go, but it was nice to meet you." She runs away.

I linger by the table guzzling my drink like it's water. The caffeine buzzes through my veins and gives me the boost I need. Checking my watch I decide it's finally time to get this over with.

Deciding to just rip the band-aid off and go for it, I head over to Danny's trailer. From the outside it looks exactly like the production truck. Clinically white with tiny windows and a rattling metal staircase.

He won't bring up yesterday, surely. He will be professional about this, just like I am about to be.

Clambering up the steps, I raise my fist and knock softly on the door. No answer. I try again more forcefully. I know he's in there, I can just tell. Finally, after knocking so hard my knuckles ache, the door swings open, nearly pushing me off the step.

Danny Covington leans on the door, his soft lips pulled into a grimace and his blue eyes glaring.

"The louder you knock, the longer you wait," he says, like a dickhead.

He slams the door in my face.

My jaw drops. *He did not just say that?*

I wasn't totally sure on the etiquette of actor wrangling, but whatever rule book I could have been given is thrown out of the proverbial window as I grab the handle and swing the door open.

Inside, the soft leather accents and black cabinets made it look more like a tour bus than a trailer. Danny Covington is lounging elegantly across one couch, holding a tablet in his hand.

"What do you think you're doing?" he asks sharply, sitting up.

"Look," I say, my anger controlling my voice box. "We got off on the wrong foot yesterday." I thrust my hand in his face. "I'm Anya and I'm just here to do my job."

He ignores my outstretched arm. "A job you are already pretty terrible at from my position."

I see red. "You're the one who apparently can't be trusted on set without adult supervision."

Danny stands, "And you're my adult supervision? I bet you've never even stepped foot on a set before. Of course you haven't. If you had, you would know that speaking to me like that was a big mistake."

"All I know is that I've been brought on this job to make sure you get to where you're meant to be."

Danny laughs incredulously. "You are so out of your depth here, freckles. You've been brought on as a pawn of my father's. Are you sending him daily reports of my comings and goings?"

"Don't be ridiculous," I snap. At least no one has mentioned that to me yet. "I am here to get you to makeup."

"I don't need to go to makeup. I'll go when I'm good and ready."

"I may not have experience on big film sets—"

"So you admit it."

"But, even I know that you need to be where you're told to go, so everyone can get on with their jobs. And right now that is the makeup truck."

He sniffs, ignoring my point entirely. "Are you saying I need makeup?"

"I'm saying those bags under your eyes aren't going to disappear on their own."

Danny basically clutches his pearls, "You did not just say that."

"Maybe they'll even give you some cucumber whilst they do your manicure."

"Hey," he snaps, "It's good to have soft hands."

I bark a laugh, "Yeah and I suppose that's an essential part of the job."

"Not for the job, " he takes a step towards me, crowding me against the counter. "I've never had any complaints."

I look up at him. He's so close I can feel his breath kiss my face. I swear his blue eyes darken.

I swallow harshly, my breath shallow. "Please." God, it sounds like a plea.

He blinks at me, his tongue wetting his lip.

What am I doing? Recovering quickly I add. "Just go to makeup. Please."

Danny catches my eye before taking a step back, "I need a coffee first."

I inhale a shaky breath. "I'll get you one." I tug my collar away from my neck, "Milk?"

"Black." Danny says, refusing to look at me.

"It will be in the truck," I throw over my shoulder, desperate to get into the fresh air. Just before my hand touches the door handle, I pull the phone charger out of my pocket and practically throw it on the counter.

The door slams behind me.

Chapter 7

DANNY

My babysitter is not very good. For starters, she's so green she might as well have been pulled off the street. Hell, they really could have pulled her off the street, I have no idea where she came from.

From the moment she dropped into the seat next to me on the train, pretending she had no idea who I was, I knew she would be a pain in the ass. I spent the whole journey trying to psychoanalyze her technique. I've met enough women — on the job and off of it — who like to pretend that they have no idea who I am. As if that was going to make me fall at their feet in gratitude for being seen me as a real person and not a character they have as their screensavers.

But no, when I overheard her phone call where she clearly had no clue who she had been sat next to, it surprised me. And then it pissed me off. Why had my father hired her? Someone who obviously had no idea what she was doing. He clearly did it on purpose. What a way to prove how much you don't care about someone, then to not care at all about the quality of staff set to look after them.

Not only is she incompetent but she's opinionated, bursting

into my trailer with her hands on her hips and a flush on her soft cheeks. God, when she backed up, basically climbing the counter, I could have sworn she wanted me to kiss her. And I could have sworn I was tempted.

The minute the door closes behind her, I rub my hands across my face. Turning to the mirror above the counter I look at my eyes. I don't have *bags*.

Sighing, I pick up my tablet and desperately try to memorize my lines. I had been sent a digital script the day after the meeting with my father, but after my cursory read, I procrastinated revising my lines.

The train would have been the perfect time to read but the whirlwind sitting next to me became an instant distraction. Her shiny hair in disarray after she pulled that ridiculous bobble hat off her head…I'd had to clench my hands to stop myself reaching out to smooth the wayward strands. And then I couldn't help teasing her, poking her to see that gorgeous blush spread across her cheeks and down the column of her throat. I had found myself wondering what else I could do to make her blush like that.

So, yeah, not much work happened on the journey.

Glancing at my watch, I try to quell my rising panic. I'm not ready for this. My heartbeat is a steady drum in my ears and I swear I can see my chest rising with my haggard breaths. My phone rings in my pocket.

"Hello?"

"How's it going?" My sister's voice is calm and brisk, and I feel myself relax.

"Fine."

Pip laughs, "First day jitters?"

"Please, as if you've never been nervous on your first day."

"I'm not a household name." Pip lies. She is just as much, if not more, famous than I am. Largely thanks to her many social media accounts, a skill that missed me in the gene pool. My social media presence consists of a retweet when the Lionesses won the Euros and a picture of a cat I saw when I was in Greece.

"Have you started shooting yet?"

I lean to peer out the window, not seeing anyone scurrying between the trailers. "I'm going to makeup soon." Where a black coffee will be waiting, hopefully.

"How's the hotel? I've been meaning to stay there." The Belle Palais is a five star hotel with a view over the Sacré-Cœur. I made my own way there last night as my so-called assistant can't seem to organize a piss up in a brewery but the grand opulence of the place is more suited to the film I'm starring in than what I would have picked for myself. But then again, having the option to pick where I'm sleeping is, naturally, out of my hands.

"It's fine," I say sharply. "Look I've got to go, they're waiting for me."

"Sure, all you need to do is remember your lines, stay out of any fights and don't disparage the family name." Pip quips, making me huff a laugh.

"I'll make sure to get on that." I hang up the phone, before grabbing my tablet and heading to the makeup truck.

When I get there, Anya is nowhere to be seen, but a steaming cup of black coffee is waiting for me in my chair.

The hair and makeup designer, Sally, introduces herself before ushering me to my chair and tucking a napkin in my collar. "It's a pretty simple set up this morning, so you won't be too long." Sally turns away from me, gathering some supplies.

"We didn't get a test run but I've been assured it will be fine," she mumbles under her breath.

I stay quiet. I would have liked a makeup test, a camera test, a costume test — I would have wanted it all. When I first started out, I used to love getting to prep with the crew, where I felt that I was a part of a team, where I could really sink my teeth into the project. Now, I'm just dumped into it the first day of filming like a child on his first day of school, disoriented and nervous.

I pick up my tablet and read through my sides. Thankfully, it's mostly non-dialogue scenes of my character working. I can manage that. Probably. A scene scheduled for later in the day is a page and a half of dialogue, so I focus on that.

Sally keeps buzzing around me, twisting my head this way and that, pulling my concentration away from the script. I can feel my irritation rising with every turn of my head. I need to get these words into my brain.

Robert: It's all here, there's no way LeCleric doesn't know about this. It's gross misconduct sure but almost certainly criminal negligence.

I repeated the words under my breath, my lips forming the words. *It's all here, there's no way LeCleric doesn't—*

Fingers moving my chin make me jump. "Can you not?" I snap.

Sally's eyes widen. "I'm sorry," she stumbles. "I need to add some Vaseline."

"Can you ask a man before you touch him?" I spat. "For Christ's sake I'm not a doll."

"No—no of course not." Sally steps back. "I think we're good here, I think you're needed in costume."

"Great." I stand and rip the napkin out of my collar. My

heavy footsteps shake the trailer as I head to the exit.

My babysitter is outside, leaning against the opposite wall and playing around on her phone. She straightens with a start as I stomp down the stairs. I look away before I can get distracted by her silky hair and dusting of freckles.

Out of the corner of my eye, I see her struggling to catch up with my quick strides.

"Costume next," she says brightly, as if the confrontation in my truck twenty minutes ago never happened.

I let out a grunt of acknowledgment.

When I get to the bottom of the stairs, she darts in front of me, damn near tripping me up in her rush to open the door for me.

I don't say a word, my jaw clenching, as I'm ushered into the truck.

Inside, the eccentric-looking costume designer guides me to a changing room at the back of the truck, and hands me a bundle of clothes. As soon as the curtain closes behind me, I slump on the rickety stool.

I can hear hushed voices outside the curtain, probably talking about what a prick I'm being.

Gritting my teeth, I pull my costume on.

When I'm ready, I emerge to allow the costume people to fuss around my body like I'm a mannequin.

"Perfect measurements," one woman says with a big smile. *Yes,* I think, *I don't know who gave them to you but I'm sure they're accurate.*

As soon as I'm excused to leave, I'm escorted by my babysitter to a waiting car, and escorted from the car to the set where cameras are being prepped. I clock a few looks from the crew but elect to ignore them, focusing instead on the sides in my hands.

Robert: It's all here, there's no way LeCleric doesn't know about this. It's gross misconduct sure but almost certainly criminal negligence.

Gwendoline Marcs comes up to me, shaking my hand and introducing herself. Of course, I already know who she is. Which is good as I will not be able to absorb any information given to me now.

Soon, I'm ushered to my mark where I listen like a good boy to the instructions from Gwen. My movements are bulky, unnatural, and *wrong.* No one seems to notice, no one shakes their heads and audibly complains about how terrible I am. No. They stare with what could only be described as confusion, and a bit of pity.

It's worse when we get to the dialogue scene. I stumble through each sentence, barking 'Line!' every five minutes, sweat beading on my forehead despite the mild weather.

Now I know the crew are getting irritated. They have started to realize what a disaster this whole operation is going to be. I'm a fish out of water, drowning on dry land under the artificial lights and the glare of the camera. They all know it.

Eventually, someone calls wrap.

I wait patiently as the sound guy pulls my mic off. He doesn't look at me, doesn't speak to me. What's there to say anyway?

I let myself be led to the transport car, to the costume truck where I pull on my street clothes. I don't look up from the floor until the car door closes behind me, ready to take me back to the hotel.

I take a deep breath and lean my head back, the city passing my window in a blur.

"Are you okay?" a gentle voice asks to my left. I start. I

hadn't even noticed Anya was in the car with me. Her big hazel eyes wide with concern.

I bristle under her attention.

"Do you have to come with me everywhere?" I snap.

"Apparently," she shakes her phone in her hand.

"Great," I mumble, closing my eyes.

I keep my eyes closed the rest of the journey, Anya's flowery scent filling the car and invading my senses.

Chapter 8

ANYA

It only takes a few days for Danny and I to find a rhythm. The disastrous first day (not including the train ride that shall never be mentioned again) has at least eased into some sort of routine. Every morning, I wait by the car outside his hotel with a cup of hot coffee. Then I accompany him — in silence — to base where I pick up the sides from production and ferry him to the makeup truck, then to costume, then to the set and then safely return him to the hotel at the end of the day.

If anything the job is well…boring.

Danny never even really acknowledges me except for when I speak to him directly, like he's an Alexa just waiting to be told to turn on. He's like a lifeless puppet on set, waiting for the director to call action before he wakes up. This morning, however, it seems Danny is determined to break the status quo.

Glancing at the time on my phone, I bite back a groan and slap a hand against the heavy wood of his hotel room door. I've never been inside the hotel, usually electing to meet him by the car, but today he hasn't emerged and I'm forced to approach the lair.

He must sleep like the dead. Unless he's just ignoring me. Unless he's…busy. Maybe there is someone in there with him, and he can't bring himself to get away.

The thought infuriates me even as it causes a strange twist in my gut at the thought. Not that I'm jealous of whoever is in there with him, that would be ridiculous. If anything I'm jealous that he's able to have a slow morning rolling in the sheets instead of waking up to a blaring alarm and multiple texts from Sarah.

Now more than a little frustrated, I start to jiggle the handle before hissing through the wood, "If you're not out here in thirty seconds I'm going to kick this door down."

"Go on then." Whirling, I see Danny sauntering down the hallway, headphones looped around his neck. So he wasn't inside with a lover. Swallowing my tongue, I take him in. Tendrils of hair stick to his forehead and my fingers twitch with the desire to brush them back. His gray t-shirt clings to his broad shoulders as beads of sweat drip down his neck.

Pulling my eyes away before I follow the droplet down to his collarbone, I glare at him, "Where have you been?"

He gives me a side eye as he comes closer, waving a hand to his attire and drawing my attention back to his tight chest. I *will not* to count the abs.

Still pressed against his door, he comes up close. Holding my breath doesn't stop me from breathing him in. Ugh, even his sweat smells good.

Reaching around me, he unlocks the door before pushing it open behind me.

"We have to be out in ten minutes, I don't have time for games," I say as I cross the threshold of his room.

"It's called exercise, you should try it."

I bristle, he did not just say I need to *work out*. "Excuse me?"

He starts emptying his pockets on the desk, glancing up at me through the mirror. "I'm just saying, freckles. You're very tense. I think you could do with some endorphins. "

"I am *not* tense."

He steps towards me. I hold my ground with a glare.

"It's not good to hold onto all that tension,"he says, his tongue wetting his lips. "Maybe you need a release." I curse myself as my heart pounds and my belly swoons. His head tilts forward and I raise my chin defiantly, refusing to look away from his eyes, even as I swear his drop to my lips.

He pulls away from me and I inhale a shaky breath.

"I'm not kidding about the ten minute warning," I say, regaining my composure but not looking up from the carpet as my feet tail him across the room. "The car is already waiting."

"Are you coming in with me?" He asks. I look up sharply and my heart stops. Mortifyingly, in my tirade I have followed him into the bathroom. Smirking, he holds my eye as he whips his t-shirt off.

Refusing to look at the muscles I already know he was hiding under his shirt, I glare at him.

"I mean offer's there," he says with a glint in his eye, his hands playing with the waistband of his shorts. My gaze drops to follow the motion and my mouth goes dry at the sight.

Swallowing, I say, "What offer?"

"For that *release*," he says with a smirk.

"Pig." I spit as I throw a rolled up towel from the bathroom counter at him. He dodges with a laugh as I spin on my heel and slam the door behind me.

My hand comes to my forehead with a less than gentle slap. *Why did I do that?* Now he probably thinks I'm a lunatic, desperate to catch a glimpse of his naked body. Although, he didn't exactly seem annoyed at the intrusion. If anything what just happened could be construed as…flirting?

Pretending to be engrossed in my phone, I wait the torturous five minutes for Danny to finish. I can hear the water running and will my mind to not picture his wet, naked body standing under the spray.

I need to get a handle on my hormones. I'm supposed to doing my job, not ogling my boss. Even if he does look really good shirtless. Even if it has been a while since I've had any kind of *release.*

By the time he emerges, fully dressed, my heart rate has yet to return to normal. Without looking at him I snap, "Lets go," and swing the hotel door open.

The car ride is silent. Logically, I know the tension filling the car and making my thighs press together is just in my head, remnants of Danny's mini strip show. If I don't look at him I don't have to worry that my dirty thoughts will be voiced. It takes all my willpower to keep my eyes from lingering on his slightly damp hair, or his soft lips or the tight t-shirt that clinging to the abs that I definitely did *not* count.

"You okay over there?" he asks, dryly.

"Hm?" I reply. "Uhuh."

"Why aren't you looking at me?"

"I'm looking at you."

"You're looking at my ear."

"It's part of you isn't it?"

"I'm sure it's irresistible but I'm sure I haven't had someone so interested in it before."

My eyes snap to his with a glare.

"You're insufferable, do you know that?"

He grins impishly.

"*Ici,*" Jaques says from the front seat.

I fling myself out of the car, desperate for fresh air instead of the lingering scent of Danny's shampoo and what I can only assume is some sort of aphrodisiac. "I'll get your sides." I slam the car door behind me.

The production truck is busy which is my first warning. I sidle up to Sarah who is frantically typing on her phone.

"Morning," I say. "Busy in here today."

Sarah grunts, "Yup. Bigwigs are here." She gestures with her head to the door separating the office to the rest of the truck.

I raise my eyebrows but before I can say anything the door swings open and a tall middle aged man walks out. His intimidating presence steals the air from the truck, his self satisfied gaze assessing the room. I try to mold into the wall to avoid the attention of who I quickly realize is Charles Covington, Danny's father. Although they don't look alike, I can see enough of Danny in his hair and frame that the relation is unmistakable.

He makes polite conversation with Sarah and Brian, or at least what I'm sure he considers polite. I pretend to be engrossed in the schedule hanging on the wall behind him, desperate to escape his notice.

"You're Danny's girl right?" the booming American voice sounds. I jump, bristling at the moniker.

"I'm his assistant, Anya," I say, stumbling over the term. Even to my ears it sounds inaccurate for my job. From his raised eyebrow, I know Mr Covington feels the same.

"How is he doing?" he asks, not quietly. I can see everyone in the small truck barely hiding their eavesdropping.

"Uhm, yeah good," I say. "He's very passionate about the

role." I know that's an outright lie. It's a struggle to get Danny to care about the job at all, but at least he's trying.

Mr Covington barks a laugh, "That's good to hear. Just make sure he shows up, alright?"

I nod. He gives me a long lingering stare, his beady eyes glistening and his tongue licking his lower lip. My skin bristles under his attention but thankfully Sarah presses Danny's sides into my hands and I'm able to make my escape.

Danny is in his trailer, leaning on the wall opposite the door as if waiting for me. I jump at his presence.

"Are those the sides?" he asks, taking them out of my hands before I can reply.

His brow furrows as he reads them, turning away from me. I shift my weight from foot to foot as I wonder how to approach the topic.

"So, uhm," I start. "I think your dad is here."

Danny freezes, his shoulders seizing up.

"I mean, he's definitely here. I just spoke with him."

Danny straightens, "I know," he says, in a way that convinces me that he probably didn't. He turns to me and runs his fingers through his hair. "How long until I'm needed on set?"

I glance at the call sheet, "Forty five minutes?"

Danny nods, "Will you run these with me?"

Huh?

I see a faint trace of red on his cheekbones. "This is an important scene and I just need to go over them with someone."

"Oh, uhm," I say. Read lines with Danny Covington? "I can see if Adriana is available?" Adriana is the female lead, and definitely more qualified for this than me.

"Freckles," Danny says softly, "Please."

Biting my lip, I gently take the sides out of his hands. "Okay, but don't laugh, I don't think I've read out loud since school." I plop on the couch in front of him, clearing my throat before I begin.

I immediately feel stupid, the lines coming out stilted and forced. It's like I've completely forgotten how humans speak. I clear my throat and try again.

"The risk is too high, no one can know."

"Is that supposed to be a Scottish accent?" Danny cuts in.

"Do you want my help or not?" I snap, flustered.

His lips shake and I narrow my eyes at him.

"Sorry, please continue."

I make a show of smoothing out the paper and we start again.

Danny knows every word of course, and the scene runs seamlessly until I trip over my words. It's worth it though, to see Danny grin at my fumbling and to see calm wash over his tense shoulders.

We finish the scene and I slap my thighs, pushing to stand up. "All done."

Before I can take a step, Danny's hand catches my arm, his large palm nearly twice the size of my wrist.

"Can we do it one more time?" He looks up at me pleading. With a huff, I sit back down.

"Fine, but I'm going to go for a Scouse accent next."

Danny makes me reread the scene until I've nearly run out of accents, so when I get a text saying the car is ready to take him to set, I'm confident he's ready for the scene.

That confidence quickly evaporates once we arrive on set and find Mr Covington lounging next to the directors chair.

The scene starts off strong, mainly because Danny refuses to look at his father. Until after the first reset, which has Danny and Mr Covington sharing a tense, loaded glance from across the room.

From that point on, disaster strikes.

I know Danny can do it backwards. He should be able to do this scene and following the run through in his trailer, nothing can really explain his need to bark "Line!" every five seconds.

Lauren, the 3rd AD is trying to be patient but I can tell by the vein popping in her forehead that she's getting frustrated. And a better word for frustrated would be pissed.

"We need to take this to Fraser, you know he isn't part of this," Lauren feeds him, calmly.

Danny clenches his jaw and nods, shaking his shoulders out.

"Okay guys, let's try this again," Lauren shouts to the crew.

I watch as his cue comes and goes, the flush in his cheeks and the tick in his jaw a pretty clear sign that this isn't going too well. In case anyone wasn't aware.

I glance around at the crew and notice more than a few eye rolls and scoffs.

My role on set is really quite bizarre, I'm not expected to do any of the jobs of the harried runners corralling crew and keeping the food stations topped up but I'm also not in any position of authority. The only authority I have is over the lead actor currently floundering under the watchful spotlight of his smug father.

I'm there to stand quietly in the corner until Danny needs me. He hasn't asked but screw it. He knows the lines, it's the goddamn shadow lingering in the back of the room and eating all the craft pan au chocolates that's responsible for this mess.

When the 1st AD yells action and I see the stubborn flush in Danny's cheek travel down his throat, choking him, I decide enough is enough.

I tiptoe to Lauren and whisper in her ear, "Can we give him five?"

I have no right to make the request but I hold firm, clenching my fingers into a fist as if I can physically stop the cameras rolling.

Lauren sighs and glances at me and nods. The next time the cameras cut she calls out, "Let's take five everybody."

"Thank you," I say quietly.

"Make sure he's on top form after the five, I can't keep people behind much longer."

I grab a water bottle from the snack table and hurry over to Danny, who is clutching his sides so close to his face his nose is brushing it.

I tap his shoulder and offer the water. He takes it without looking at me.

"Okay, what gives?" I ask softly. "We ran these earlier and you know it, I know you do, you could say it in your sleep. Hell, we ran it so many times even *I* could say it in my sleep at this point."

"I know," he snaps, his attention drifting to the back of the room. Mr Covington isn't even paying any attention, instead laughing loudly with the producer.

"It's because he's here," I say, gently.

"You don't know what you're talking about. It's too damn hot in here," he snaps, tugging at his collar.

I look around at the airy room, the high ceilings relieving any trapped heat.

"There are a lot of people in here I suppose," I placate.

"One less if you leave," he says, not looking up from the crinkled paper in his hands.

I glare at him *"The risk is too high, no one can know."* I'll be saying these lines on my deathbed in 70 years time, most likely.

He takes a deep breath and spits *"We need to take this to Fraser, you know he isn't part of this."* and suddenly he's off, reciting his lines perfectly. He speaks the lines so quickly, he hardly even realizes he's done it until I can't stop the smug smile spreading across my face.

I laugh, "I told you you could do it. Ignore him, the sooner you calm down, the sooner we can get this scene wrapped and he can be on his first class flight back to LA and out of your eyesight."

He blinks in surprise and then rolls his eyes, holding up a hand. "I'm not thanking you."

I pretend to think about it, "That feels suspiciously like a thank you but sure."

He shoves me playfully, gratitude shining in his eyes. He doesn't look to his father once as he crosses back to his position.

I wander back to Lauren, "He's ready."

Lauren is immediately back in action, "Okay everyone back into positions were going to run it again."

Danny does it in one take.

Chapter 9

DANNY

As Anya had predicted, my father had boarded the first flight out of Paris the morning after his set visit and as his plane took off so did the weight crushing my shoulders.

Two weeks into filming and I'm finally settling into the role, the lines coming naturally to me and the character taking over the working part of my brain the second Gwen yells action. Every day, Anya appears outside my hotel with a hot black coffee in hand and croissant flakes dusting her shirt. I remember one morning, my previous assistant Eric had spilled ketchup from his breakfast sandwich on his shirt and I made him change before I could even look at him. But with Anya, I find myself itching to dust the crumbs from her clavicle with the tips of my fingers. Thankfully, I have resisted the urge so far.

When Anya stormed into my hotel room, practically joining me in the shower, I don't know what came over me. It was the easiest thing in the world to flirt with her, tease her until that pretty blush spread across her cheeks. The minute the door had slammed behind her, I tried and failed to regret my actions, and only the cold water snapped me out of it.

Today, she's leaning against the car as usual, coffee cups in hand. I take mine from her outstretched arm and slide inside. As soon as I settle in, I look over at Anya who has her nose buried in her phone.

"You'll probably get twenty minutes before we have to get you to makeup." She knows I need some time to relax before getting dressed up like a show pony. "So you can have some time to hide the horns before anyone important sees you." She looks up and gestured to my hair and nonexistent devil horns, her eyes sparkling with mischief.

"Funny." I deadpan, trying not to touch the top of my head.

She giggles and returns to her phone, "It's the new guy's first scene today, he plays Russell Jones. He's *'Robert's nemesis who wants to sabotage the plan.'*"

"I have read the script, thanks," I say dryly. "Who's playing him?" I haven't familiarized myself with the cast or crew list, and I obviously didn't have any chemistry reads. Even for me that's a rarity. The director usually pushes to get me to read with prospective cast — even when I'm a done deal. They like to make sure I have some spark with my co-stars. My father has already handled my scripts, my schedule, my *measurements*. I have no doubt that his word on casting was final and it didn't matter if it worked for me.

If I'm being honest with myself, I can't even bring myself to care. This ride is already on the tracks and it's too late to get off now so I might as well get on with it. I know Anya, and Gwen and whoever is playing my scene the day of, and that's enough.

"Callum McBride."

I instantly stiffen. *Callum McBride.*

I haven't seen him since the party at Cassie's Malibu mansion. The night I punched him so hard he fell through a glass table dusted with coke and he cut my lip with his plated signet ring.

"That's who's playing Russell?" I ask quietly, my ears ringing.

Anya's head snaps up. "Yeah, looks like a last minute casting." She looks at me quizzically. "Is that a problem? Do you know him?"

I look at her incredulously. Sometimes it surprises me how little Anya knows about me. I'm so used to everyone knowing everything there is to know from Twitter or a vague blind item. Or at least thinking they know everything.

"We have…" Beef. "A history"

Anya nods and bites her lip. "Is it going to be a problem?"

I'm shaking my head before she's finished talking and the lie tumbles out of my mouth without warning. "Nope."

"Okay." She looks skeptical.

"We're here," the driver announces, in accented English.

"*Merci*, Jaques." Before Anya has climbed out of the car, I'm already hustling to my trailer.

I feel Anya behind me but before she can step over the threshold I spin, "Twenty yeah?"

"Uh, yeah?"

I close the door in her face.

In the trailer I pull my phone out, dialing his number before I can talk myself out of it.

"McBride. Are you fucking kidding me?"

"It took you this long to notice?" The chuckle my father has at my expense makes my teeth grind. "Just what I thought, you have no care for the job at all—"

"Have you upgraded coke for crack? Why the hell did you think this was a good idea?" I spit.

"Listen," Charles says, I can imagine his neck getting red. "It was a last minute addition and we're announcing it this week. The buzz is going to be immense."

"The only thing that's going to be announced is my exit from this shitty little film."

My father snorts, "You'll do no such thing."

"I'll walk off right now." Before I ever have to work with a snake like McBride.

"You leave now, don't be surprised by tomorrow's headlines."

I pull the phone away from my ear, my fingers clutching it so hard it might snap in half. The thinly veiled threat makes my blood boil. I don't even bother to ask what he'll 'leak' to the tabloids. My father likes to use the threat of leaking stories to the press. It's his way of keeping me in line. He can tell them anything and they'll print it. Foursomes with escorts, destroying priceless artwork, selling meth to children. Even if I swear till I'm blue in the face that it's all fake, no one will believe me and I'll be slaughtered in the court of public opinion.

I grit my teeth. "Tell him to keep his mouth shut. He does his lines and he fucks off. I will not put up with this bullshit."

"Do I look like that pretty little babysitter of yours?" Charles asks. "The day to day has no interest to me. Grow up and do the job you're being paid to do, Daniel."

I pull the phone away before I have to hear that man hang up on me. I pace the small length of my trailer, making the room shake with each heavy step.

My fingers hover over the call button, but I don't click. Sitting on the couch, I contemplate calling. I know if I speak to Pip my anger will just send her spiraling and she'll either panic or cry. Neither of those options are particularly appealing.

I could just not mention it to her. What is she even going to do about it anyway? She's in New York in fittings all week, she might not even hear when it comes out in the press. I could call her later, when I have the time to sit and talk through it with her, hopefully with a cold beer in my hand and Callum McBride off my set.

Taking a deep breath, I steel my nerves. If I don't tell her as soon as I know, she'll be more upset later finding out I kept it from her.

Me: Callum McBride is in this.

Pip must have her phone in her hand because her text bubble appears immediately. It keeps disappearing, a clear sign she doesn't know what to say.

Pip: Did you know?

Me: I just found out. Charles is behind it.

The bubbles again.

Pip: Don't do anything stupid.

I won't do anything he doesn't do, I think to myself.

Me: I won't.

Pip: Don't make it a thing.

Me: I'm going to speak with Gwen and get him kicked off.

Pip: I guess Charles thinks the attention will help revenue, right?

Me: Pretty much

Pip takes so long to reply I think she must have left her phone.

Pip: I want this to go well for you Danny. If this helps the film and helps YOU, I will live with it. I won't even be involved really. I just need you to keep cool about it.

Me: Pip, I can't keep cool around that prick

Pip: You'll have to.

Me: I've got to go, they need me over here.

I throw my phone with frustration, taking a deep breath.

Fuck this, I don't care what Pip or my father says, I'm not having that man on my set. Just thinking of last year, when I held my little sister as she sobbed over that piece of shit, makes my decision final. No, he's not staying.

I fly out the door and down the metal stairs, nearly plowing into Anya as she clutches my daily sides in her hand.

"Hey, I was just bringing these—" I storm past her. "Where are you going?"

I ignore her and hear her footsteps keeping up with me. She doesn't even know where we're going but it feels almost like she's got my back.

I storm up to the production truck and swing the door open without knocking.

Gwen, Michael, and Rachel sit around desks, littered with paper and half-eaten breakfasts.

"Danny?" Gwen asks, startled. Anya slips in behind me and quickly closes the door from prying eyes.

"Callum McBride." My jaw hurts from how tightly it's clenched. "I won't work with him. If you keep him, I'm walking."

They all glance at each other warily.

Gwen starts uneasily. "Look, I know you two don't have… the easiest of relationships."

I scoff and cross my arms across my chest.

"But it looks really good for our backers." My father more like. "The buzz—"

"If I hear one more word about the fucking buzz I will throw something."

Rachel pipes up, "At the end of the day, he's signed his contract and we've already started shooting studio shots back in the UK. The only way he'll get out is if he leaves voluntarily, and from what he's said that doesn't seem likely."

"Then I'm out," I say. "Burn my contract right now. I don't give a shit."

"Your father—"

"I don't give a *fuck* about my father! Hang him for all I care." My arms spread wide nearly touching the sides of the cramped production truck. Anya is pressed against the door of the trailer, her eyes wide and shocked, her eyelashes brushing those damn freckles. I must look like a madman. I blink, her wide eyes arresting me in my tracks. I take a calming breath and turn around.

Before I can speak, Michael says "Your contract is ironclad. You're not getting out of it."

"I'm sure my lawyers would have something to say about that."

"We'd sue you for breach of contract."

"I'll sue you for dangerous working practices." It's only a matter of time before McBride's poison seeps through the set.

"You're not here to have an opinion on who we hire. Your job is to show up and read lines."

I huff a sarcastic laugh, "Well, you can get anyone to do that. I can't hear any more of this," I turn and storm out the trailer. "Anya, get the car."

"Danny." I hear Gwen call behind me. I don't care.

Chapter 10

ANYA

I feel like I'm most likely missing some important information but now is not the time. I jog to keep up with Danny as he makes long strides to where Jaques is usually waiting with the car.

"Jaques has gone on a pick up," I tell him belatedly. He can't hear me, his fury rolling off him in waves.

I jump to his side and gently steer him back towards his trailer like a sheep dog. He doesn't notice.

"I won't work with him," he spits. "I don't care what they say."

I keep my mouth shut.

He doesn't notice when I corral him to his trailer, stretching my arm to open the door for him. He looks around confused as he takes in his new surroundings.

He turns to leave but I block his door.

"Let's just cool down a minute okay?" I say, raising my arms. He glares at me.

"I don't need to cool down," he says, glowering. "I need to get the fuck off this film."

"Well, Jaques is not here right now and I'm sure security

would mow you down if you try to leave like this." I doubt security would do anything except wave goodbye but it's all it takes to get Danny to just sit and think for a minute.

He backs off and slumps on the couch like a deflated balloon, the fight leaving him.

"Right," I say. I don't know what to do with this new Danny. We're usually spitting venom at each other. I'm not used to his ire being pointed in a different direction. "Do you want to talk about it?"

He shakes his head. "It's a long story." He points at me in an afterthought. "You steer clear of Callum McBride." He says sternly. "Especially after I'm not here. He's not a good guy."

"Yes, *dad.*" That earns me an eye roll. He leans his head against the wall and I sit beside him. "I can't imagine I'll have a job for much longer if you leave." I try not to consider the possibility too much. It was nice whilst it lasted.

He rolls his head to look at me. I didn't realize how close we're sitting until I can feel his breath brush against my cheeks.

His eyelashes twitch as they scour my face.

He closes his eyes and takes a deep breath. He's quiet for a few moments. "Fine." He says with his eyes still closed. "I'll stay."

Really? Well, that was easy.

"Are you sure?" I ask.

He runs his hand over his face and gives me a half convincing nod.

I bite back my smile. I don't know what I did but it worked. *Excellent work, Anya.*

"Go back to the truck and say that I've been ranting and throwing stuff around in here but that you talked me down. I want minimal contact with him outside scenes. No rehearsal, no bumping into him at the food truck, no chatting in between takes. He shows up does the scene and then fucks off again."

"Should I be writing this down?" I ask.

He shoots me a look. "And I mean it, freckles. Stay away from him."

I nod once. If just the thought of him being on set causes this reaction in Danny, I have a pretty good inclination to steer clear.

I go to stand and do his bidding but his strong fingers clasp my wrist. I glance at where our skin touches, tingles racing up my arm at the contact.

"Wait a minute," he says, hoarsely, his finger brushing the sensitive skin on my inner wrist. "Make it believable."

"Okay," I sit back, not pulling my arm away from his. We both stare at our hands. I'm scared to move, scared to breathe, scared to spoil whatever this is.

My phone chirps, spoiling the moment. I disconnect from him as I scan the text from Rachel.

Rachel: Come back to the truck

Rachel: Alone

"That's my cue," I say standing. "I won't be long."

I leave Danny where he is, his eyes burning into my back as I go.

As I cross the base to the production truck, Jaques pulls up alongside me. I wave to him as he stops the car and he returns with a smile. A tall blond man stumbles out the back. His eyes are hidden behind dark sunglasses and he has a jumper tied around his neck like he's just jumped off his jet from the Hamptons.

This must be the infamous Callum McBride.

He pulls his sunglasses off and I hurry away before he has a chance to say anything to me. Even if Danny hadn't warned me to stay away I would have felt the smarmy energy wafting off the man in waves.

I hurry up the steps and give a perfunctory knock before letting myself in.

Rachel looks up from her desk. "What's he saying?"

I sigh heavily as if I've finally escaped a very delicate conversation. "He's really angry, but he has agreed to stay and finish filming."

Relief washes over the truck. And I thought I couldn't act.

"But he has some conditions." I relay Danny's instructions to a chorus of scoffs.

"God, why do these actors think they own the whole film? I hate bending over backwards for these pricks." Rachel groans.

I can't decide whether to be defensive on Danny's behalf or glad she's including me in her bitch session, like I'm part of the crew. I don't fit in right with the cast or the crew, always a little bit apart. The only place I fit is with Danny.

Gwendoline sighs, "Well at least you got him to calm down, Anya." I blink before realizing she's addressing me. My cheeks heat and I nod shakily.

I can't believe Danny's meltdown is what's finally caused Gwendoline to speak directly to me. *She knows my name*, I think faintly.

Michael throws his hands up and says "Fine" like it's anything but. He turns to Rachel, "We'll need to throw out today's call sheet. Which one do we need more today? Danny or Callum? God, this is going to be a ball-ache."

Rachel sighs, shuffling the papers on her desk and pulling out a red pen from her desk drawer. "I'd probably say Callum. He's here now and we can pick up Danny's scenes tomorrow."

"Right, fine." Michael says briskly before turning to me. "Get him off the lot and we'll see you tomorrow."

Chapter 11

DANNY

All of my righteous anger at McBride for what he did to my sister, my father for his threats, production for forcing my hand, slipped away as soon as Anya said she would be out of a job. I couldn't let that happen. I've already done enough to make her life difficult, getting her fired just because I can't to do what I'm told? I would deserve the vitriol I'd bring on myself in that case.

The trailer feels too big without Anya sitting beside me and a dull headache pulses behind my temples. *Get it together*, I tell myself, willing the anger to leave my body. I made my choice. I chose her.

Still unable to shake off the buzz in my blood, I cross to the counter and rummage until I find a scrap of paper, a page ripped out of an old script draft.

Clutching a pen between my fingers, I scrawl across the page. Words and stanzas bleeding through the page from the force of my hand. I fill the page quickly, barely reading the words before I take a breath. My emotions pour out of me as a melody forms in the back of my mind.

Once I run out of paper and the muse escapes me, I rise

from my crouched position and take in the disjointed words in front of me. I hear the song as I scan the lyrics and it feels *right*.

The sound of a car door closing outside the trailer snaps me out of my trance. The paper clutched in my hand suddenly feels foreign. The words that had flown out of my mind instantly makes me recoil. Embarrassment cramps in my stomach. Did I actually just do that? Did I try and *write* my anger out like I can do it that easily? Like there's any point in sending those jumbled, incoherent emotions out of my head and into the world? The delusion that gripped me so suddenly is quickly replaced by crippling shame.

My trailer door bangs open and I crumple the paper into my pocket.

"Well, it's all fine. There's no rush but it's probably best if we make a hasty exit." Anya climbs the metal steps poking her head through the door. "Why do you look like that?"

"Like what?" I ask, my mouth dry.

"Like you've just run a marathon."

I unglue my feet from the floor and grab my hat from the chair. I press it firmly onto my head as if I can physically restrain the thoughts tumbling around my skull.

I can't look at Anya as I follow her into the waiting car.

I lean my head back on the seat and close my eyes. It's barely noon and I'm exhausted. My fingers twitch on my knee, tapping out the rhythm that held me in such a frenzy. I clench my fist.

We pull up at my hotel and I say a gruff thank you to Jaques as I step out of the car. I keep my head down as I cross the marble lobby. It's only when I'm waiting for the elevator do I notice Anya has followed me.

"Jesus," I snap, jumping about a mile out of my skin.

"Sorry," Anya winces. "I thought you might need something else. I can order you some lunch or something?"

I stare at her blankly.

"It's lunchtime and we left before catering."

"I'm not hungry."

Anya bites her lip, "Okay. I'll let you get some rest."

The elevator arrives. I step one foot inside before Anya says. "Oh wait!" She rummages in her bag and emerges with a small packet in her hand. "I keep them for emergencies."

I take it from her warily. It's an old packet of French biscuits, the ends crumpled and faded.

"Just in case." The faint hint of pink on her freckled cheeks is like a soothing balm on my racing thoughts.

"Thanks."

"It'll all be okay, don't worry." The smile she shoots me is dazzling.

The elevator doors close between us.

It's only later, when I collapse on the couch in my room and take a bite of a crumbling biscuit, that I take the paper out of my pocket.

Chapter 12

ANYA

The first day Danny and Callum are on set together is already a disaster. I'm a big believer in signs so as soon as the camera cards corrupt and they have to change the kit, we might as well all go home.

The tension is already high from the arrival of Callum, and Danny's unprecedented freak out. I have already heard whispers of his Diva-ism, which had started to die down once Charles had left us alone for a few weeks. Danny was quiet when I took him home that first day. He didn't say anything in the car and didn't even say goodbye when we got to his hotel. The days following were much the same. I could cajole him out of his moods most of the time, but it was like trying to get a stone to bleed. Or laugh.

If he wants to be a child about it, he is more than welcome. He can treat me like a coat rack for all I care. So what if there was that…moment in his trailer before he agreed to stay. It almost felt like he changed his mind…because of me? I decide to just log that with all the other moments that have raised the hair on the back of my neck and caused a swoop in my belly, and just forget about it completely.

He hasn't spoken to me today. I've kept it up as long as I could without saying anything, but unfortunately, this job relies on communication — even if it is one-sided.

I linger outside his trailer, psyching myself up to confront the moody bastard. The June sun is beating down on me and I curse myself for forgetting my sunscreen. I have maybe five minutes before I turn into a lobster.

Get over yourself, I think in Danny's direction in his tin can, before huffing up the steps to his door. Before I can even reach the top step the door swings open, nearly knocking me out. Danny emerges, and he doesn't even acknowledge my near death experience before he's backing me down the stairs.

"There's a delay on set." I hurry after him as he strides towards makeup. "You don't have to be in makeup for like twenty minutes."

"We can just start early." He doesn't even look at me.

"I mean, if you want to un-corrupt the camera cards yourself, then sure? Otherwise I think we're at the whims of the camera loader."

Danny ignores me and stomps up the steps of the makeup truck, pulling the door open.

"Danny," I reach for his arm but think better of it.

His large body blocks the doorway so I can't make out the faces of the girls inside the truck but I hear their startled gasps. Danny ignores them and sits in his usual chair.

Sally steps up, wringing her hands and glancing at me for support. I throw my hands up in the universal *I don't know what the fuck is going on* sign.

Sally glances at the call sheet taped to the wall and the big red cross covering it. À la the camera cards. "Danny, you aren't supposed to be here for another twenty minutes."

Danny glances around at the empty truck before settling into his chair. "I'm here now."

Sally glances at me again. Chewing my lip, I glance at Danny. Yes, he is being a prick right now, but he won't even look at me. Something is going on. So, I pick a side. "Is it okay if you do him now?"

Sally looks to the ceiling before throwing her hands up. "Fine."

Danny doesn't even acknowledge us, pulling out his phone. He's probably just looking through his settings, the loser.

"I'll uh," I mutter, "I'll go let production know."

Sally glares at me as I make my hasty escape, her eyes screaming, "*Coward*".

Stepping into the fresh air, I start to panic. You can't just decide when to start filming, that's just not how it works. The thought of telling Rachel that the lead actor has decided the shooting schedule almost makes me break out in hives, but the thought of going back in there and telling Danny to leave is not an option.

Fortunately–or unfortunately–I spot Sarah outside the food truck typing on her iPad. Taking a deep breath, I approach certain disaster.

"Uh, Sarah?" I ask

Sarah replies with a vague "Hmm?"

"Yeah, so Danny is in makeup right now." I say, gesturing to the truck behind me.

Sarah's brow furrows, glancing at her watch. "Why did you do that? He's not supposed to be in makeup for another twenty minutes."

"Yeah, so I know that, and also he knows that. But he—uh—well he doesn't seem to…care." I finish lamely.

Sarah looks at me blankly. "What?"

"Yeah, he seems really keen to uh, get rolling."

"Right, so I will go and tell the director, and the DOP and the sound guys and the art department that Danny is ready to *get rolling*." She says it so flatly that the words swallow me whole.

Humiliation burns my cheeks but I have nothing to say. My teeth bite into my lip hard enough to sting.

"I thought your job was to handle him," Sarah says. "So handle him. We're not starting any earlier." She strides off muttering under her breath.

My lip will be chewed off by the end of this shoot, and I am going to send my plastic surgery bill to Danny Covington's door.

Shamefaced, I return to the makeup truck but linger outside for the rest of Danny's time. When he finally emerges, I can't even look at him, my embarrassment at getting told off hardening into fury in my gut.

Fuck this man thinking he can treat us all like servants, ready to obey his whims at the snap of his fingers. My fury morphs into resolve as soon as Danny opens the door. I stand with my arms crossed and what I hope is a fierce glare.

Danny doesn't even acknowledge me as he brushes past me in the direction of the costume truck. Unlike my earlier hesitance, I have no qualms about grabbing his arm and pulling him to a stop. I will jump on his back and tackle him to the ground if I have to.

He glances down at my arm with an indistinguishable look on his face.

"Your trailer is that way," I say, not bothering to point.

"I'm going to costume."

"Not for thirty minutes you're not."

"They'll be ready for me."

"No, they won't."

"Yes, they will."

"No, they won't."

"Look I haven't got time to play this game with you, freckles."

"*Au contraire*, you have buckets of time, thirty minutes in fact."

Danny rolls his eyes. "Give me a break. I'm being a good boy and ready to get this over with. You should be happy."

"I'll be happy when you just do the things you're supposed to do when you're supposed to do them."

"I'm going to costume."

"They're not ready for you, Danny. Go sit in your trailer until it's time."

Danny glares at me, his arms crossed over his chest. I stand my ground, ignoring the biceps bulging out of his t-shirt.

"You're very bossy, do you know that?"

I shoot him a toothy grin that doesn't quite reach my eyes. Huffing a breath, he stalks off in the direction of his trailer. I follow behind him, gloating in my win. He closes the door behind him.

Message received, I think. I detour to find Sarah and tell her that Danny is back on schedule. Sarah doesn't thank me, obviously, so I make myself scarce. Heading to the food truck, I grab a banana.

Jess is pouring what looks like a dozen cups of tea from the vat.

"Can I help?" Jess jumps, spilling some tea out of the small disposable cup. "Sorry."

"It's fine," Jess laughs nervously.

I start placing the lids on the cups, hoping she has already got a system to remember which is which.

"Thank you," she says, piling them into a carrier.

A young guy reaches between us and pours himself a coffee. "Hey Jess," he glances at me. "Danny's girl."

I raise my eyebrows. That's a nickname that I'd rather not catch on.

"Anya," I say, striving for politeness but not quite making it.

He leaves without a word.

"Sorry," Jess says, awkwardly.

"It's fine. I'm not offended." Lie.

"I need to get back to *Danny*," I say, emphasizing his name as if to prove a point. Although what that point is I can't say.

Jess ducks her head and goes back to her tea as I head back to the truck. *Danny's girl.*

I feel a touch of guilt for snapping at Jess, she's not even the one who said it. I rub my eyes, praying this shitty day is the result of a bad dream.

I've meandered long enough that by the time I get to his truck, Danny is right on time. He swings the door open before I can even knock.

"Am I on time now?" he asks sarcastically.

"Precisely." I smile. I expect it looks more like a grimace but he doesn't seem to notice. His foul mood settling over both of us like a dark cloud.

He's already made me look bad in front of Sarah, I snapped at Jess and even the sound guy thinks I'm just his bitch. Throughout his costume fitting, I stand fuming against the wall. I'm so angry I don't even allow myself to acknowledge that he is basically naked behind the thin curtain separating us.

On set, I settle into my corner and watch as Gwendoline speaks to Danny. Usually he nods or looks at her or in some way acknowledges what she's saying, but today he stands stone faced and still.

Callum McBride swans onto set. From my research, Callum is a heartthrob in his own right, coming up through the TV route and jumping over to film after his last show went viral. Largely because of his good looks and fueled by rumors of a liaison with his married co-star.

As soon as Danny spots him, all the tension that's been rising in him this morning finally pushes to the surface. His jaw clenches and his shoulders hunch. Seeing the two in the same room, it's understandable why Charles wanted to push this. Callum is tall and blond, and looks like he just stepped off a yacht. Though standing next to Danny, Callum McBride's good looks pale in comparison. A few inches shorter with a wider face and a cruel smirk.

I begin to get the feeling I probably shouldn't have left Danny alone to stew earlier. Whatever bad mood he was in has just intensified during the time he sat sulking in his trailer. The notion proves to be pretty accurate after one hour rolls into two which rolls into four.

It's pretty clear that Callum is a classic agitator. Every time they yell cut, Danny's expression shutters but Callum's grin climbs along his cheekbone as he mutters something too quiet for the crew to hear.

As time goes on, I notice the crew getting restless. Every time the DOP pulls away from the camera he grimaces, and every time the boom operator pulls his arms down he sighs audibly. There is no way Danny is unaware, but it's like his attention is warped by the blond acting opposite him.

Gwen and Rachel huddle and I can immediately smell trouble.

"Alright guys listen up," Rachel announces, "We're looking to go into grace to get this done."

Groans and shuffles fill the room. Grace is essentially fifteen minutes of overtime. *Unpaid* overtime.

Danny doesn't notice.

The hair and makeup trainee, Katie, creeps onto set and heads for Danny. I'm moving before I even question why.

The question is answered as Danny explodes, "Can you back the fuck off? Jesus Christ."

Katie nearly drops the concealer brush in her hand. I step up and put my hand on her elbow, steadying her as I feel her arm tremble. I glare at Danny.

"Hey man, back off," Jerry, one of the crew, says.

"Oh piss off mate," Danny snaps, his face scrunching. "Go back to your corner."

"*Danny*," I hiss, stepping in front of Katie.

He doesn't acknowledge me, still staring over my head at Jerry.

Rachel forges into the fray. "Is there a problem here?"

"Yeah there's a problem," Danny seethes. "I'm surrounded by fucking idiots."

The grumbles of the crew get louder and the animosity bubbles in the crowd. I feel tethered to Danny's side. It's clear to me what side I'm going to end up in this fight, no matter how infuriated I am.

Eventually Gwendoline pipes up. "Alright everyone let's cool off. We'll forget the grace, I think we have enough."

I see Callum hide his smirk behind his hand.

Katie finally backs away, ungluing her feet from the floor.

I turn to Danny. "Let's go."

Danny clenches his jaw and storms away, shrugging off the hand I place on his arm and giving Callum a wide berth.

The walk across set is terse, the ride back to base even worse. My anger whirls in my belly, tinged with embarrassment. All day I've been fending off criticism and scorn because I've been saddled with a belligerent man child who can't even be a decent person to Katie, who is easily the sweetest girl on set.

Danny slams the car door behind him as he heads to his trailer. I hasten my strides as I chase after him, catching his trailer door before he can slam that too. I'm going to have to replace it with a curtain just to stop him taking his feelings out on the poor door frame.

"What is going on with you today?" I ask incredulously.

Danny ignores me, pulling off his shirt. I glance away at the sight of his broad back, refusing to acknowledge the dip in my belly that should be full of righteous anger.

Recovering, I say, "You've been in a foul mood all day. Just tell me what the problem is and I can help."

"Would you just piss off, Anya? I don't know why you think you're helping me because you're not. You're just making everything worse. I don't give a shit about this vanity project, I hope I waste enough money to bankrupt the whole fucking lot of them."

I clutch my hands at my hips, my frustration from this horrendous day finally spilling over.

"You might not give a shit about this job but every single other person here does. They're away from their families working grueling hours before you even get out of your thousand euro a night bed. They work hard all day whilst you lounge in here, and they have to stay and work longer when you are being completely selfish just to piss off your father."

"It's pretty cushy for you in this trailer too though isn't it?" he seethes. "All you do is buzz around my ear and fetch me my fucking coffee."

I see red. "You know what Danny? Fuck you."

"Fuck me?" he laughs scathingly. "Original."

"Don't you patronize me, you stubborn prick. I'm here running around after you, getting treated like a social fucking pariah on set, and for what? A shitty credit working with a pretty shitty person. You know when I got this job I thought I had finally had my big break? But it's all fucking pointless. I have a pointless job. But every single person out there is working really fucking hard for this *vanity project* and you just offended every last one of them. You're pathetic. You need to grow up and appreciate what opportunities you've been given because there are thousands of people who would not be so careless with theirs."

I finish my rant, heaving. Unable to even look at him, I turn and slam the door behind *me* for once.

Chapter 13

DANNY

Having to organize getting back to my hotel without Anya's constant presence feels like a low point. Even Jaques barely acknowledges me when I slide into the back of the town car.

I yank my hat off and run my hands through my hair, trying to take a calming breath. I close my eyes but all I can see is the look on Anya's face as she tore me a new one, hands flying and those hazel eyes blazing.

I pinch my eyes with my fingers until I see spots, trying to dissolve the image I can't get out of my head.

Resting my head against the cool glass of the window, the streets pass by in a blur. We pass the entrance of a park, the tall green gates flung open as cyclists glide through the opening.

"Can you stop?" I ask, swallowing against my dry throat. "Please."

Jaques doesn't say a word as he pulls to the curb. I hardly wait for the car to stop before I've stumbled onto the pavement, pulling my hat back on my head.

My shoes crunch in the dirt pathway as I wander through the park. I barely look up from the pale sand beneath my feet.

Everyone was right. Everything anyone has ever said about

me is right, I proved it all back there. I lashed out at a trainee who shook like a trapped field mouse. I lashed out at her, but really I was angry at myself. At myself for letting Callum McBride get under my skin now the same way he did months ago. For allowing him to goad me into a fight, leaving a glass table shattered on the floor and my reputation in ruins. McBride's doing it again. Over and over. And I let it happen every time.

As soon as I saw McBride, that night replayed in my head. His cheek underneath my knuckles and the look in my sisters' eyes. It's like a bad dream he's determined to make me relive.

I collapse on a green chair, startled by the sharp backwards angle that makes me slide back until I'm almost horizontal in a public park. The move surprises a laugh from my throat. As if I could pity myself more.

I gaze up at the trees above me, the gentle swaying distracting me from my pool of self loathing.

Couples walk by holding hands, children ride past me on bikes. I stare at them, envious of their lives. Their ability to walk through a park without worrying about prying eyes. I pull my hat off in frustration, yanking my hair between my fingers.

Pulling it back on to rest over my eyebrows, I lean my head back against the metal chair with a thud.

Anya's face swims before me, her angry glare and flushed cheeks. The minute I met her, her sharp words bathed over me like a fresh start. No one has spoken to me like that. They've always thought their opinions, hidden them behind phone screens, but never said directly to my face. I almost can't help myself now, from needling her, just to see what she'll say.

But today, it wasn't a pleasant experiment. It was a harsh

truth. I put so much effort into resenting the people who think badly of me, that I end up proving them all right.

It's not anyone on that production's fault that I'm there. None of them hired me. None of them leak my name in the press and spread lies about me — although they probably will now. All they've done is do their job, earned a living, and I've been stomping around like they all owe me something.

How many people do the hardest jobs in the business just so people like me can demand an extra window in their trailer or specifically orange M&Ms on standby? Would I even be in this job if it wasn't for my parents? Yes, they pushed and pushed me in this direction, but did I really have to let them?

When I was starting out, it only took my father a few calls to get me an audition for *Better You Know*, and the producer was a woman who used to come to my mother's dinner parties. I worked hard on that job, but all of that ambition has left me since then. Yet, I'm still working because my father keeps hiring me.

The garden is getting busier now, the after work rush settling in. I remember that day in my father's office and feeling envious of the corporate people on their lunch breaks. I wanted to be them, I wanted to have a job that meant something, that wasn't just playing pretend. But how many of those people wish they were me?

For such an opinionated woman, Anya has yet to be wrong about anything. I take a deep breath and stand, crossing the park in long strides.

A fountain stands in the center of the park, toy boats bobbing in the water controlled by a group of giggling children.

A green shack stands nearby selling snacks. I join the queue, keeping my head down. The last thing I need is someone to spot me when I'm deep in self reflection about my life choices.

The queue moves slowly and my neck starts to hurt. By the time I make it to the front of the line, I quickly remember I can't speak French.

"Uh," I say dumbly. Anya would know what to say. I hold my fingers up and point to the picture of packaged ice creams. *"Two of deese."* The man scoffs at what I now realize was just English with a strong fake French accent. I'm an actor for god's sake.

He hands me two ice cream bars and I mumble a quiet *"merci"* as I pay. I know that at least.

I hold the plastic packaging between my fingers so they don't melt as I head back to Jaques.

He's standing against the car door, dutifully waiting for me. He's tall and broad. I've never seen him standing before which explains why I never imagined he'd be the size of a defensive linebacker.

He pulls the door open on my approach but I shake my head and close it.

"Would you like one?" I ask, holding out the two bars.

His eyebrows raise. "Uh, okay."

He takes one but waits for me to open mine before he does the same.

We stand quietly and gaze into the park through the tall gates, happily munching on ice cream.

"Do you like your job?"

Jaques looks at me, confused, and I wonder if he doesn't speak English. Anya always speaks to him in French so it is possible.

"I love my job," Jaques says in accented English. "It's what I love to do."

"Bet you get a lot of assholes in the back don't you?"

"Sometimes," he shrugs. "Sometimes they buy me ice cream."

I huff a laugh as part of my ice cream falls off, hitting my palm before I catch it in my mouth.

When we're done, I take his wrapper and throw it in a nearby trash can. He holds the door open for me and I meet his eye as I say "*Merci*."

He sends me a friendly smile in return, "Back to the hotel?"

I wish I could ask to be taken straight to Anya, to turn up at her door and beg for forgiveness. Anything to see the disappointed look in her eye replaced with her familiar sparkle.

"Yeah, to the hotel." I say, pulling my phone out of my pocket. I hover over her number, but instead I click on the browser and pull up a search.

"Hey Jaques, do you know of any good florists?"

Chapter 14

I drag myself onto set the next day, bleary eyed and grumpy. The coffee I drank this morning is already wearing off and Claudette does not believe in travel mugs so it's been a solid thirty minutes without a caffeine fix.

When I pass the burly security guard I greet him with a quiet *"Bonjour"* and he very enthusiastically responds. He must not have been here for the clusterfuck that was yesterday.

Shrugging it off, I head towards the craft table. Danny isn't needed on set until noon but Sarah requested I be here for breakfast before picking him up. God knows why. To punish me probably.

When I get to the craft table I find an overflow of pastries, macaroons and the sweetest tarts. Standing at the end handing out croissants and biscuits, looking far too perky for a seven am call time, is Danny Covington.

I blink in surprise, convinced I'm still dreaming. But there Danny is, standing next to the caterer organizing treats and chatting to the crew.

Nothing at all like the man from yesterday.

Finally, he notices me staring at him. He smiles slightly and inclines his head. Passing the cheery crew I sidle over to him. He turns towards me and reaches under the table.

"I figured you'd be too tired to make it to the bakery this morning so I saved you some." He hands me a cup of hot coffee and a little brown bag with a pain au chocolat inside.

I take both offerings silently. "What's with the career change this morning?"

He gently touches my elbow, guiding me further away from prying eyes. "I thought a lot about what you said yesterday and you were right. I wasn't thinking about it, everyone else who has to work longer and harder than me. And I wasn't very nice."

I raise my eyebrow.

"I was a stubborn prick," he admits, a self-deprecating smile pulling the corner of his mouth. I smile into my coffee. "So I thought I'd do something nice for the crew. It's not much but I wanted to do something." A faint blush touches his cheeks as he dips his head.

"It's nice," I say softly. "You'll probably have to do this for a while though so they know you're sincere."

He laughs, "I know. I might just open my own bakery now, to get ahead of the game."

I sip my coffee. The harsh words of yesterday are not forgotten despite the warmth spreading through my belly — from the coffee and something else I refuse to acknowledge.

"I'm sorry that I've been hard on you. I get that you're just doing your job." He looks me in the eye. "I'll do better."

I bite my cheek and look away. "Well, thanks. And I am here, if you, you know, want to talk about anything." I scuff my foot on the gravel.

"I know you are, freckles," he says softly.

The earnest look on his face almost takes my breath away.

I purse my lips. "Make sure you wear a hairnet tomorrow. I don't want to find a hair in my croissant."

He laughs, "You got it."

I shove him back towards the table where he's welcomed with friendly jeers. I smile before slipping away.

Stepping into the makeup truck, I immediately spot Katie sitting in one of the chairs.

"Hey," I say gently, nervous after yesterday's debacle.

"Anya, hey," Katie says brightly. "You alright?"

"Yeah, I just wanted to see if you were okay?" I didn't expect to find her in floods of tears but I thought she'd still be a little shaken up.

"Oh, she's more than okay," Sally says, returning from the back of the truck. "She got a nice little pick me up this morning."

Pink spreads across Katie's cheeks.

"Oh?" I grin.

Katie's eyes dart to a bouquet of flowers on the counter.

"A secret admirer?" I ask nearly squealing.

"No!" Katie protests blushing.

Sally laughs, "Your Danny knocked on the door first thing this morning with those and an apology for acting —what was it he said Kate?"

"Like a daft pillock," Katie says with a giggle.

"That sounds about right." I touch the pink petal gently, a soft pride settling in my chest at the thought of Danny surprising the trainee with a bunch of flowers.

My Danny.

Chapter 15

The morale on set is significantly lighter after Danny pulls the stick out of his ass. Tensions stay high whenever Callum is on set, but Danny does his best not to let his niggling get to him.

Today is my first day off in what feels like weeks and I feel like a spare part without Danny to follow around all day. I clean the whole apartment, even polishing the bare kitchen cupboards. It's not even eleven o'clock.

Slumping on the couch and pulling out my phone I send a text to Danny.

Me: Everything okay?

The phone buzzes in my hands.

Danny: Why are you texting me?

Lovely. I roll my eyes and ignore his reply.

I debate checking in on Rosie so I swipe through her Instagram story. Looks like she's at our favorite brunch spot in London. Why am *I* not having brunch in London?

I wallow in my pity before it hits me. I'm in Paris and I'm lounging on the couch wishing I was in a different city. Shaking my head I stand and rush to my suitcase (which is still half packed) and pull on the red polka dot dress that I packed with no reason to wear.

I swan out of the heavy front doors and onto the quiet street, the heat rising from the pavement. I slip my sunglasses over my eyes and feel lighter than I have in weeks.

I wander with no intention until I eventually stumble upon more crowded streets. The Seine glistens in the sunshine and I stop and take photos to send to my mother. The narrow alleyways of the Latin Quarter create a maze that I meander through, dodging tourists and waiters enticing me into their restaurants. I feel the muscle memory kicking in as I walk up the steep incline that leads to the grand blue dome of the Pantheon.

I used to come here with my mum and Claudette. Inside, I would hang over the banister and watch the Foucault pendulum that shows the earth's rotation, mesmerized by its constant motion.

Once I turn the corner, I take in the building in all its glory. Definitely not one of the most famous sites in Paris, but popular enough that it's still be considered a tourist hotspot.

I make my way up the boulevard towards it, debating whether to go inside. One look at the queue and I quickly change my mind, instead, opting for sitting at one of the cafe tables opposite, where I can have the perfect view as I drink coffee from a mug and not a styrofoam cup.

A waiter appears. *"Bonjour, manger ou boire?"* he asks in a monotone voice,

I order a coffee and a croissant before sitting back and soaking in the June sun.

I watch the hustle of the street from my small table and pull my phone out. I take a few pictures of Pantheon, and then without thinking, turn my attention to the people. An old lady leaving the bookshop opposite, a stack of books under her arm, a glamorous woman striding down the street wearing stylish sunglasses, a young couple talking quietly together at the bus stop, a young man in a baseball cap staring at me mouth agape. I lower my phone blinking.

Across the road and staring right at me is Danny Covington.

Once our eyes meet I quickly look away but not before he crosses the road and heads my way.

"Are you stalking me?" I ask as soon as he is within talking distance.

He laughs, "I'd ask you the same thing." I squint up at him as he stops in front of me. His usual attire of dark jeans and plain t-shirt is familiar, but the bright smile on his face is not one I'm used to.

"I don't remember inviting you," I say pointedly as he settles into the chair opposite me.

"Must have missed it," he says cheekily. "What are you doing here?"

"What are *you* doing here?"

"I'm exploring."

"Well I'm exploring here, go explore somewhere else."

He smiles at me, as the waiter arrives with my espresso. He looks up at him. "I'll have the same, please." The waiter bobs his head.

I roll my eyes. "We can't spend every second of the day together, it's not healthy."

"We don't spend every day together, just Monday through Saturday."

"It's Sunday."

"Yes, so this doesn't count." Danny chuckles. "Come on, I won't ask you to do anything for me all day. Not one single thing." The waiter returns with Danny's espresso.

I drop my head back.

"So what shall we do?" he asks, taking my silence for acquiescence. I look at him flatly. "Come on, what shall we do?"

"We–" I gesture between us, "–won't be doing anything."

"Come on, it's not like either of us have anything better to do with our day." He spreads his arms as if lounging in a cafe is not very much doing something.

Who is this man? He's nothing like the grumpy, snappy actor I've known the past few weeks.

"Speak for yourself." I throw a balled up napkin at him and glare. I try to get the attention of the waiter which is, typically, impossible.

Eventually one saunters over with a pompous "*Oui?*"

"*L'addition, s'il vous plait.*" I say.

The waiter nods and wanders off.

I look through my bag hunting for my purse.

"Come on freckles, we can do boring things you want to do like go take photos of strangers."

I give him a scathing look, before returning to my rummaging. I look up when I hear a beep, Danny is removing his card from the card machine with a knowing smile. "Well it seems you owe me lunch."

Ugh.

"Fine, we can walk to the next place together but then you go back to the hole you crawled out of and leave me alone."

"A few hours and you'll be begging me to stay."

"It doesn't even take thirty minutes to get to where we're going."

I get up and walk away. Danny comes up beside me. I take

a moment to appreciate the new dynamic we've slipped into. I'm usually the one doing the chasing. I lead him away from the Pantheon and down the hill.

"So, do you bring headphones on these walks?" he asks, putting his hands in his pockets.

"No, of course not," I scoff.

"Don't scoff as if that's a stupid question. Everyone listens to music as they walk."

"But then you don't soak in the atmosphere."

He laughs. "I'd argue that you absorb more atmosphere whilst listening to heartbreak ballads."

"That's not how you *flaneur*."

"Bless you."

My eyes will most likely roll out of my head by the end of the day.

"I'm only playing. Come on, what's a flaneur?" He butchers that so it comes out *fl-egh-ne-uh*.

"Thank god you don't have any lines in French."

"It'd just mean you'd have to help me run them."

"Thank god you don't have any lines in French." I repeat, smiling sweetly.

"You haven't answered me, what's a *flan-her*?"

I sigh. "It basically means to wander around, look, take in the surroundings. The Parisians are experts at looking, it's like the whole point of Paris and why all the buildings are so beautiful and the cafes have seats facing out, so people can observe strangers."

"Like stalkers."

"*No*," I say exasperatedly. "It's just a way of life — here." I pull out my phone and show Danny a black and white image of two men in trench coats with their hands behind their backs smoking cigars.

He nods, taking it all in.

"I've got it." He says seriously. I take the phone back and walk on only to realize he is no longer behind me. I turn and see him ambling behind me with his hands behind his back and his purple vape hanging in his mouth like a cigar.

He looks up, and pulls the vape from his mouth pensively. "I must say zee architect-teur is *magnifique*."

I laugh, the sound making him grin around his ridiculous vape.

"I'm *flaneuring*!" He says

I pull the vape from his mouth "You're an idiot. And these are bad for you." I say as I take a drag of the sweet smoke. He smiles.

"Better than crack," he jokes.

I hand him back his vape. Why did I do that? Our lips just touched the same thing. We basically just kissed! I can't bring myself to look at him as I speed up.

"I've never done it, you know. Crack." I glance up at him, surprised. Where did that come from?

"Oh I—"

"I only stick to the posh people drugs. Like cocaine."

The glint in his eyes tells me he's joking so I slap him gently on the arm as we amble through the gates of the Jardin de Luxumbourg.

"I like your hat and sunglasses." I say "Very *celebrity in disguise*."

He laughs. "Yeah I sometimes think that it's less of a disguise and more of a glowing neon sign saying 'hey this guy thinks he's being sneaky.'"

"Would you even wear a baseball hat if you weren't famous?"

"Nah, it doesn't suit my jawline."

I roll my eyes. "That jawline gets a million likes on Instagram."

His smirk grows. "You follow me on Instagram?"

Feeling heat rise through my neck, I scoff. "Oh please, you just come up on my explore sometimes."

He raises his eyebrows as if to say that he knows I'm lying.

"Do you think *paparazzi* will be around?" I ask flustered, gesturing to his get up.

He adjusts his hat. "Unlikely, this is more for if a random fan with a phone spots me. Paparazzi rarely come unless called."

I blink "Is that true?"

"Oh yeah, whenever you see a celebrity papped it's usually orchestrated by them so they can sell clothes or whatever."

I mull this over. "Do you call them?"

"I don't but sometimes my agent does. Or my parents. Especially if we're all together — they love getting the family shots."

"That's annoying."

"Yeah, it just sucks when I just want to hang out with my sister. We usually just have to order sushi in or something. But yeah we can almost never go out all together."

I nod. I can't comprehend never having any privacy when hanging out with family and having to stay in and—

"Wait, did you just say you order in sushi?"

"Yeah, why?"

"Ugh," I groan dramatically. "I was actually feeling bad for you for a second then and then you ruined it. *Sushi.* That's the most rich boy takeout ever."

"What!" He exclaims. "It's very affordable now, everyone eats it."

I peel into laughter "Yeah, from Yo Sushi, I bet you get a five star restaurant to send a waiter with a fresh china plate."

He doesn't answer.

"You do!" I howl. "Just get a pizza like the rest of us, you psycho."

"Right, well I'll take you to Nobu and then you'll change your tune."

My laugh gets caught in my throat. That sounds like he wants to take me to a restaurant. Just the two of us. Like a *date*.

Desperate to avoid thinking about that for too long, I scan our surroundings. "Here, here's something better than sushi."

I pull him towards a créperie stand with bright blue shutters leaning open.

The hot plate near the window is an excellent sign. "What do you want?" I ask him.

Danny squints at the menu, "Is this not just a plate of sugar?"

"Of course not," I scoff, "You get a little bag to eat it from."

He chuckles, "I'll have what you have."

I turn to the man behind the counter

"Bonjour, deux chocolate crépes, si'l vous plait."

I see him reach for his wallet and stop him with a hand on his arm.

"Oh please, put that away."

"Let me, freckles," he insists.

"Absolutely not. It's eight euros, calm down."

I hand my euro over to the man in exchange for two juicy crépes.

"Now we're even," I say as I hand him his crépe.

I watch as he takes his first bite, gripping it tightly in his hands as he closes his mouth around it. His eyes flutter and I swear I hear a…moan? Suddenly feeling very hot, I focus on my own crépe. No way am I salivating at the sight of Danny eating a crépe. I sound like the worst half-French pervert ever.

Taking a deep breath through a mouth full of chocolate goodness, I gather my composure enough to ask, "You like it?"

He groans in agreement.

For god's sake, he needs to start verbalizing before I collapse on the ground in a puddle.

I clear my throat. "Yeah I love these. My grandmamma used to make the best sugar crépes but she always used to say the Paris ones were the best. Even though it's touristy, she always said it was worth it."

"Smart woman," he mutters.

"The biggest red flag is if you see they already have a pile of premade crépe that they just reheat." I shudder. "That happens in the touristy spots so keep an eye out for that," I tell him seriously.

"Understood." He nods "If I see it happen, I will be sure to spit on them."

"As is right," I nod around another bite. I concentrate on not letting the melted chocolate run down my palm. I look up to see Danny staring right at me.

I lick my lips, heat flushing across my body.

Who knew crépes were an aphrodisiac?

Turning away I say, "Let's go this way." I march ahead, scoffing my crépe down so we can move past whatever is flowing between us.

Chapter 16

DANNY

I didn't expect to find Anya when I left the hotel this morning but thank god I did. After she gave me the tongue lashing I rightfully deserved, things have been awkward between us. I don't know when things changed, but the idea of her disappointment in me suddenly became a strong motivator.

McBride is still getting under my skin, but he manages to do it in a way that no one else can notice. It will just be a sly comment under his breath between takes that sends my blood pressure rising. And then I snap at him and end up looking like the bad guy.

I feel like I'm drowning under the whole thing. Relentlessly being prodded and poked and stared at. Watched with weary glances waiting for the inevitable breakdown. It's all crushing. If I'm set up to fail, what's the point in trying?

When I woke up in my hotel this morning, paid for by production and picked out by my father, I felt the walls close in. I was itching for en excuse to leave, to get out before the door sealed me in forever, when I had a text.

Anya: Everything okay?

I was stunned. Everything was very much not okay but how

did she know that? Was she messaging me out of duty or was she genuinely asking? I had to know.

Me: Why are you texting me?

I had stared at the phone in my hand, willing it to buzz with her reply. The longer I waited, the more I realized how ridiculous I was being. She was just doing her job, she didn't actually want to have contact with me outside of it. Refusing to wallow in my gilded cage, I left the hotel intent on taking my mind off the job and the girl.

Which didn't work. In her dark red dress and sipping a coffee, Anya looked like a dream. A dream my mind crafted to distract from the empty feeling in my chest. I felt like rubbing my eyes just to be sure she was really there. I couldn't resist talking to her, seeing her eyes light up with challenge as I needled her.

I could have left her alone. Her words were asking me to but her eyes…her eyes wanted me to stay. Sharing playful banter with her has been the highlight of this whole ordeal. I couldn't walk away from her even if I tried.

Now, as I watch her out of the corner of my eye as we wander through the streets, I can't help but be thrilled that she listened to me.

"Where shall we go now?" she asks me, a far cry from her reluctance to be seen with me earlier.

I smile. This whole day I've felt lighter than I have in months. Joking around and playing with Anya —I feel like a different person.

"Let's go get a drink," I say. The sun is already setting over the Seine but I don't want the day to end. The thought of sitting in a restaurant makes my shoulders hunch. I think we've been inconspicuous so far, constantly on the move. I don't particularly want to sit so openly where anyone can see me, but the thought of leaving Anya now is out of the question.

"I have an idea," Anya says, taking my arm. I love when she touches me like this. Guiding me without thinking. She can take me anywhere and I'll follow.

She pulls into a small store and leads me straight to the wine section. "Red or white?"

She crouches down to read the bottles on the bottom shelf, her crimson dress billowing around her. "Red," I say, dazed.

Anya grabs a bottle from the shelf and then wanders across the aisles grabbing a baguette and a block of cheese. I take them all from her, cradling them in my arms precariously. As we make our way to the check out, we pass the stationary aisle. Out of the corner of my eye I spot a stack of small blue notebooks, small enough to fit in my back pocket. Anya walks ahead oblivious as my feet halt on the linoleum. Shifting the groceries in my arms, I quickly grab a book off the stack and follow her to the cashier.

I unload our stuff onto the conveyor belt, hiding the notebook under the cheese. Anya goes to pull out her purse, but I stop her with a hand on hers. No way am I letting her pay.

She rolls her eyes but doesn't argue. She puts the food in the canvas bag on her shoulder and I quickly put the notebook in my pocket.

Anya leads me through winding alleyways until we cross a busy street. We don't turn left or right, instead, Anya finds an opening in the tall brick wall that lines the river. I follow her down uneven steps until we reach the path that wanders along the length of the Seine. The sun is starting to set over the horizon, bathing the water in flecks of gold. Small crowds of people linger along the cobblestones, sharing glasses of wine and perched on picnic blankets. No one looks up as we pass. It's perfect.

Anya finds a spot against the wall. She plops down and extends her long legs in front of her. The hem of her dress brushes the tops of her thighs and my mouth goes dry. I settle down next to her. I can't keep myself from sitting close, pressing my denim clad thigh against her bare one.

She gestures for the bag I have with the wine and snacks. She takes the wine bottle as I peel off a chunk of baguette. The soft bread melts in my mouth.

Anya swears. "You don't have a corkscrew do you?"

"I don't usually carry one, no."

"Well shit," she says, chewing her lip and contemplating. "Give me your shoe."

"My shoe?" I ask, amused.

"Yes, we'll bash the end of the bottle until the cork pops out."

"And that will work?" I ask, unlacing my trainer.

Anya shrugs. "I saw it online once." She takes the shoe I hold out and starts smacking it against the bottom of the bottle. I try not to laugh at her look of concentration as she spanks a wine bottle with half of a pair of Reebok trainers.

"Stop laughing," she hisses. "You try."

She shoves the bottle and my shoe into my hands.

"Why don't you just see if one of the people around here have a spare we can borrow?" There are a lot of things I would do for this girl, but this is probably my limit.

"Why don't you ask?"

"You're the one who speaks French."

She rolls her eyes as she pushes to her feet. There's a smattering of dust on the back of her smooth thigh from the ground and I have to sit on my hands to stop myself from brushing it off.

I watch as she approaches a group further down the bank. She gestures with her hands and the woman at the front nods as she hands over a corkscrew. Anya says something which makes the group laugh and she waves as she walks away.

"Pass it here," Anya says, standing over me. My eyes are level with the hem of her dress as it flutters in the wind. I can't take this anymore. It's like I've never seen legs on a beautiful woman before.

I pass over the bottle and she uncorks it easily. She returns the corkscrew to the group and I wait for her to settle before saying, "We don't have glasses."

"Ugh." She groans dramatically, slumping against the wall.

I laugh and place my hand on her thigh, "We can just share, freckles." Her soft skin under my palm is inviting and I can't help myself from brushing my fingers against her smooth skin. Her eyes widen at my ministrations, her mouth parting.

I could easily lean forward just slightly and capture those lips with my own.

"Here." I hand her the wine and watch as she brings the stem of the bottle to her mouth.

"Have you ever done this before?" she asks, looking away.

"Drink wine out of the bottle?" I ask, taking it from her. "Once or twice."

"Very funny," she replies. "Have you ever worked in Paris before?"

"I haven't, but I've come with Pip for Fashion Week a few times. Not my kind of thing usually but it was alright." I look out at the setting sun as it bathes the banks of the Seine in beautiful pink and gold. "What about you? You worked here before?"

"No," she says. "I came here to visit my aunt once or twice as a teenager but then my mum stopped speaking to her and I haven't been here since."

"What did they stop speaking?"

Anya shrugs. "I have no idea. I was too young to get it and it's too late to bring it up now. Although, mum did reach out about using Claudette's apartment so who knows? Maybe they'll make up."

"What's your mum like?"

"She's one of a kind," Anya smiles. "She's a French teacher so she's always complaining about her students, but I know she loves it."

I see her open her mouth ready to ask about my mother so I jump in with another question before she can.

"So what do you want to do next? After the film, I mean."

She takes a swig from the bottle and glances at me out the corner of her eye. "Marry rich."

I laugh and gently nudge her shoulder as I take the bottle for myself, deciding not to think too hard about who her rich husband could be. "I'm serious."

Anya sighs and looks out on the glimmering river.

"Honestly?" She shrugs. "I don't know what I want to do. I picked this job when I was seventeen and now I'm twenty four and I've barely done anything. This is my first professional job and I'm on babysitting duty." She glances at me. "No offense."

I smirk. "None taken."

"I don't know. I feel like I placed all my eggs in one basket when I was a teenager and now I'm trapped. Back then I wanted to be a director but now I don't even know if that's a genuine life goal, or a dream I just came up with as a child with no concept of what the job actually was or how to get there."

"You don't want to work in film anymore?"

"It's not that. Or it is. I don't know." Anya leans her head back on the wall and reaches her hand for the wine. I pass it to her. "I guess I'm still working it out." She takes a sip from the bottle. "What about you?"

I snort. "What about me?"

"Will I be seeing you at the Oscars one day?'"

I laugh. "I doubt it."

"What are you talking about?" Anya exclaims. "You'll definitely get one one day."

"Maybe if *Better You Know* has a sequel." It has the desired effect when Anya giggles. I want to record the sound and listen to it every day.

Once her laughter dies down, her smile causing her eyes to crinkle in the corners, the words tumble out of me. "I feel the same."

She looks at me, confusion etched on her face. "Trapped."

Her eyes study my face, searching for the lie.

"Well, what would you want to do?" She finally asks. "If you could do anything."

I laugh, rubbing my hand across my face. "I don't know."

"Come on, there must be something. Selling whiskey, hosting a podcast—"

"Music." I blurt out. I pinch my eyes shut. I can't believe I just said that.

"That's a great idea! Composing your own music?"

I gape at her, my head tilting in a jerky nod. This conversation has run away from me. I never thought I would confess this side of me, let alone to my bossy assistant. What are the odds she'll let this go?

"Is that what you've been writing in your trailer?"

Not likely to let it go then. I'm stunned.

"What?" she asks, fidgeting. "Was it a secret?"

"No," I say, quietly. "I've never tried to hide it, but no one has ever noticed."

I take a swig from the bottle.

"You didn't have music lessons or anything?"

"Oh, I had lessons. My father was all about making sure my education was well rounded. But it was made very clear to me that I had one avenue to take and that was this one."

"So, you were forced to act?"

I nod. "I wasn't forced, more like I was put on this path and then all of a sudden I couldn't get off it again."

"Do you like acting?"

I let out my breath. "I don't know if I like any of it. But it's been brought to my attention that millions of people would kill for my job, so I can't complain too much." I watch as a faint blush rises beneath her freckles.

"Well, there must be something you like about it."

"I like this job." I rest my head against the wall and turn to look at her. The setting sun picks up the reddish strands in her hair. I could spend the rest of my life picking out the rust color strands.

Suddenly, Anya stumbles to her feet.

"Where are you going?"

"Uhm," she says, her hands flapping. "I had a cramp."

I raise an eyebrow and catch her flailing hand. My fingers smooth down to grab her wrist. I gently tug until she's back down with me, but the force of the motion almost pulls her into her lap. She readjusts at the right moment and collapses next to me, close. Too close.

"We haven't finished the wine," I say softly.

She nods and swigs the rest of the bottle. I would be impressed if I didn't think she was trying to distract herself. "Music right?"

"Music?"

"I've heard of somewhere near here. Let's go." She stands again, holding her hand out as if to pull me to my feet. I don't need her help but the prospect of holding her hand is one I won't give up easily.

Chapter 17

ANYA

That wine has gone straight to my head. I don't know where my inhibitions have gone but they must be floating in the Seine by now. All day we've been talking and laughing and… flirting? And now he's *holding my hand* as I take him to Cavette de Huchette, a cavernous jazz bar with dim lighting and dark corners. What am I doing?

We get to the club and Danny stands behind me, finally letting go of my hand as I order entry for two people. Before I can get my money out, Danny has reached over my head and handed over his card.

I look up at him. "Are you ever going to stop doing that?"

He winks and doesn't reply. My breath hitches, as he places his hand on my hip and guides me through to the bar. He orders a bottle of champagne and two glasses, but I don't offer to pay for this one — if he wants the expensive stuff, that's on him.

Danny grabs the champagne bucket, handing me the glasses. He takes my spare hand again and leads me down the winding stairs at the end of the bar. Holding his hand is almost awkward as we carefully make our way down the old, narrow staircase but I can't bring myself to let go.

The cavern-like room is cold except for the heat of the bodies swaying on the dance floor. Danny leads the way through the crowd, tugging me behind him. I nearly lose him but grab onto his pinky finger as we squeeze past the dancing couples.

I sidestep to avoid an old man with a shock of white hair underneath a straw hat spinning a young woman in his arms. The woman squeals with delight, glancing at her friends in the corner who are cheering her on.

I assume Danny is leading us to the plush leather seats lining the walls but instead he twists towards me. The movement is so sudden that I glance behind his broad shoulder looking for a camera phone pointed our way.

"Who is it?" I ask, dragging my eyes back to him.

"Huh?" he asks, leaning down to hear me over the music as he places the champagne on a nearby table.

I tilt my head up to reply but anything I was meant to say gets stuck on my tongue. He's so close I can feel his cool breath on my cheek. Our noses are nearly touching. Before I can pull away or move closer, Danny raises our hands, seamlessly turning his hand so he's cradling mine instead of me clutching his finger. Not once breaking contact.

Confused, I glance back at him as he curves his arm around my back, pulling me flush to him.

"Dance with me," he murmurs.

My hand moves to his shoulder. "I don't know how," I say quietly. Despite the roaring music and the crowd, I fear speaking any louder will burst the bubble we're hiding in.

"I'll show you." He sways me in his arms, in time with the slow jazz the live band is crooning. My hand inches further across his shoulder until my fingertips brush the warm skin of his neck. Danny's eyes flutter closed.

My heart is pounding, not from the dancing — which is really more of a coordinated swaying — but from the hard chest pressing against my front. I'm trapped in his azure eyes. His tongue pokes out between his lips, sweeping across his bottom lip. I look back up at him, my mouth going dry.

His warm palm lowers until it's indecently resting at the base of my spine.

I take a deep breath in, leaning my head towards him, begging for those final few centimeters to disappear and his lips to be on mine.

The band changes the song to an upbeat swing number, which is more suited to a post-war ball room than whatever charged atmosphere we have created in our own little world. Danny blinks and steps back, a sly grin stealing across his mouth.

Before I can open my mouth, Danny straightens his arm and sends me spinning away from him. I yelp as I attempt to gracefully spin like the other dancers on the floor. He pulls me back to his chest and I giggle, the tension from earlier dissolving into laughter.

Danny continues to spin me on the dance floor, our intimate dancing forgotten and replaced with terrible attempts to swing dance. He spins me on the dance floor until my cheeks hurts from laughing. We escape the crowd to down the champagne, before spinning back onto the floor.

Eventually, when the champagne runs dry and the band starts to pack up, Danny pulls me towards the exit.

"Home time," he murmurs in my ear as we step out into the street.

I fumble with my phone, and order a car, automatically sending it to his hotel.

I step away from him, the cool evening air sizzling the heat from my body. The car arrives immediately, and it's second nature for me to clamber in the back seat beside him. If Danny thinks it's strange, he doesn't say.

The ride to his hotel is quiet and goes by far too quickly. When we pull up in front, Danny pauses with his hand on the door. "You coming?" he asks, his voice rough.

I gulp. "I'll come make sure you get in safely."

Danny nods, his eyes darkening. He runs around the back of the car and pulls my door open for me. Flustered, I step out and take his waiting hand.

He doesn't let me go as he tugs me through the lobby of the hotel and into the elevator.

On his floor, the elevator doors clang shut behind us. The dim lamplight in the hallway illuminates his face, leaving the gentle stubble on his jaw in the shade.

Suddenly nervous, I push my hair behind my ear and turn to him. "Well, I can safely say you're back in your room."

He nods and then looks back at his door. "I'm not technically inside yet."

"No."

"Maybe you should just, y'know, wait to make sure I'm inside. Safely."

"Ye—yes. Just to be safe." I'm barely breathing.

He turns and unlocks the door, peeking over his shoulder. I don't know where to look, so I admire the rouge wallpaper decorating the corridor. I'm just doing my job, escorting him home. That's all.

He opens the door and turns to me. Our bodies are less than

a foot away from each other. If I take one little step forward I would be inside his hotel room. Another step and the door could close behind me.

"It's not very safe," he says, his voice thick. "Until the door's closed."

I clear my throat. "Right."

He takes a shallow breath, his eyes darting to my lips. I lick them nervously, my heart beating in my ears, and I take that tiny step. He swings the door closed behind me.

Our bodies are pressed together now. I stand still, afraid to move, afraid to speak, afraid to acknowledge this moment. I can feel his warm breath on my cheek.

He raises his hand, slowly, as if giving me time to move away. My feet are heavy and weighted to the floor. My body is frozen, caught in the taught air between us. His hand slowly brushes against my cheek, placing his hand behind my ear.

"It's safe now," he says, softly.

I look into his blue eyes, the pupils dark. My breath catches in my throat.

"I should leave," I whisper.

"Yeah," he replies, leaning in. His face is so close to mine now, our lips a millimeter apart.

"I mean it," I say, in what I hope is a stern voice.

"I know."

My lips crash into his. The kiss is soft at first, and when his tongue tentatively skims the edge of my lip, I melt into him. I open my mouth wider as my hands creep up around his neck. His arms encircle me, pulling me into his hard body. With a groan, he deepens the kiss and the ache between my thighs is undeniable.

I tilt my head away from him, attempting to catch my breath.

"We shouldn't."

His lips slowly travel down to my neck, biting and sucking on the soft skin. "We are."

I can't argue with that. I thread my fingers through his hair and pull his lips back to mine. The gentle kiss of before is forgotten as our mouths collide.

"Bed," I mutter in between kisses.

He smirks against my mouth. "Still so bossy."

I ignore him as he slowly starts to move us backwards towards the bed, his fingers sliding up my back, gently caressing the underside of my breasts through the thin cotton of my dress.

The back of my knees hit the bed. I fumble with the hem of his t-shirt and pull it up over his head, breaking our kiss.

"Fuck," I mutter, running my hands over the places I've been dying to touch. His skin is smooth and golden, a fine smattering of hair that I run my fingers through. In a moment of insanity, I lean forward and press wet kisses along his chest.

"Your turn."

He starts kissing my neck again as he works my dress up my thighs. I stop his hands, suddenly nervous. "I don't—I don't exactly look like a model."

He pauses and looks into my eyes. "I want to see you freckles. Please."

My knees nearly collapse as he presses a final kiss to my lips before he pulls my dress over my head. His eyes darken as he stares at me, practically licking his lips before unclasping my bra. "Fuck Anya." He swallows.

He kisses a path along my skin, tracing the freckles across my chest until he reaches my aching breasts. He sucks one nipple into his mouth as I bite back a moan. My heart stutters as he peppers my skin with hard kisses and gentle bites, worshiping my skin. He pushes me to lie back and hovers over me. He leans down to kiss me as his hand explores my body, grasping a nipple between his fingers before tracing down my stomach to the edge of my underwear.

I whimper as his fingers find the bundle of nerves begging for his attention, his deft fingers teasing me.

"It's not enough," I breathe, fumbling with his belt buckle. Before I can unclasp the button he slips a finger inside me and I think I go blind.

I'm barely able to keep kissing him as my breath is robbed from me with every flex of his finger. He presses wet kisses to my neck and I feel his teeth brushing my skin.

My hands tug at his jeans, hoping he gets the message to pull them off but he presses his hand deeper inside me. His thumb joins in his ministrations and my body lights up, tumbling into an orgasm with a gasp.

He presses a kiss to my lips as I open my eyes drowsily. "Anya."

Impatiently, I tug at his jeans until he finally stands and strips off the remainder of his clothes. His cock springs free and my mouth waters at the sight. He leans to the bedside drawer but I can't help myself. I sit up and take him in my mouth.

"Fuck," he hisses, his hand twisting in my hair. He's bigger than I expected, as I widen my jaw and flick my tongue across his delicate tip

He brushes my cheek with his finger and gently pulls out of me. He cradles my head in his hand and tugs his thumb against my swollen lip. I look up at him under my eyelashes. "I won't last if you keep doing that, freckles."

He fumbles in the drawer, emerging with a condom that he takes no time at all to roll on. I fall onto my back as he hovers over me, his lips reclaiming mine.

I feel him nudge at my entrance and I wrap my legs around him, desperate to feel him.

"Please," I beg. "Fuck me."

He moans as he pushes inside me, his head burrowing in the curve of my neck. His hips flex as he tortures me, the pressure building and building until I hit my second climax, so soon after my first. As soon as I come down from my high, he pistons inside me desperately, following soon after with a groan.

I wrap my arms around him as I try to catch my breath, pressing a kiss to his hair.

I slide off him and fall into the cradle of his shoulder, resting my head against his pounding heart. His fingers trace up my arm, pebbling goosebumps in his wake. Before I have a chance to overthink, to catch my breath, my hand flattens against his chest descending lower and lower until he shifts. Towering over me, his eyes scan my face. Through hooded eyes, I return his stare. His hair mussed from my fingers.

He takes my lips in a kiss that burns through the night.

Chapter 18

I open my eyes to a strange buzzing. Reaching my arm out to my bedside table, I'm met with soft flesh under my palm.

I jerk my head up. There underneath my outstretched fingers is Danny Covington. My wayward hand is resting by his nipple and — *oh my god, I licked that,* I realize with mounting horror.

Flashes of the night before flood my head. My mouth on his lips, my mouth on his sculpted chest, *his* mouth everywhere.

Realizing my hand is still resting on his chest, I swiftly yank it back but before I can, Danny catches it. He brings our joined hands to his and presses a kiss to my knuckles. I finally allow myself to look at him and he shoots me a lazy grin.

I almost —*almost* — melt at that burning look in his blue eyes but the buzzing starts again.

"Shit," I curse, flailing out of bed, the bed sheets wrapping around me as I search for my phone. I yank the bed sheet tighter around myself and start rummaging through the pillows scattered across the floor. "Jesus, are we in a H&M home?" I curse under my breath.

I hear a chuckle from the bed but refuse to acknowledge him.

Finally under a wayward sock, I find my phone and answer with fumbling fingers.

"Hello," I gasp into the receiver.

"Anya," Sarah says sharply. "Where is Danny? He's needed on set like, yesterday." Quickly checking the time on my phone, I swear silently and bring the phone back to my ear.

"Uhm," I say, turning to face said man laid across the bed like a naked Adonis, smirking and stroking his rapidly growing cock.

Heat rises to my cheeks as I battle my increasing panic and that infuriating streak of arousal. "I'm outside his room now, trying to wake him up."

I pull the phone away from my ear as Sarah drones on about call times and grace periods.

Danny strokes his impressively large erection and my face burns red hot. My eyes snap back to his face where he sports an annoying smirk, noticing where my attention has lingered.

Heart racing, I tune back into Sarah's diatribe. "Everyone is getting antsy, Anya. We can't start the day without him."

I grab a pillow off the floor and throw it at Danny, knocking his hand away from his cock. He laughs, the smug prick.

"I hear you, reception is on their way up now with the spare key. We'll be there in half an hour."

I click my fingers at Danny and furiously gesture at him to get out of bed. Smirking, Danny rolls out of bed and heads to the bathroom in all his naked glory, but not before pressing a quick peck to the top of my head as he passes.

Wait, what?

"He better be in this makeup chair in thirty minutes, Anya." Sarah snaps, before hanging up.

I throw the phone onto the bed and run my fingers through

my hair, taking a deep breath.

I slept with Danny Covington last night. *The* Danny Covington. Famous heartthrob and troublemaker, the star of my first big break Danny Covington. My *boss* Danny Covington.

As I hear the water running, I try extra hard to regret last night but…I can't. I knew exactly what I was doing, and so did he. We were scratching an itch, getting it out of our systems. Getting it out of our systems multiple times. Now we can just move on with our lives like reasonable adults.

Determined, I locate my dress and yank it on.

Danny returns to the bedroom in a cloud of fog. Thankfully, dressed. He leans against the door and watches as I pull my trainers on.

Refusing to look at him I say, "Good, you're ready. I haven't got time to go home and change but no one saw me yesterday so it should be fine."

Danny nods seriously and then says, "What are you going to do about that hickey?"

"What?" I dart to the mirror. There on the juncture of my neck and shoulder is a purpling bruise, made by Danny biting down as he thrust deep — nope, not going there.

In vain, I try rubbing to see if it will come off. Cursing myself, I frantically run my fingers through my hair as I announce, "If anyone asks, I'll just say I met someone. They don't have to know it was you."

Danny comes up behind me, his arms encircling my waist. "If I hear you give the credit for this to anyone other than myself," he says, pressing his lips to the tender flesh. "I'll mark you again and sign my name."

My breath shakes as my pulse flutters beneath his mouth,

my thighs clenching involuntarily. His tongue peeks out with a tender flick.

Reluctantly, I pull away from his arms. "This cannot happen." I try to take a step away but his arms rest on the desk, caging me in.

"It's already happened," he smirks.

I glare at him through the mirror.

"What can't happen?" he asks.

"This." I gesture between us. "Us."

"Oh really?" he says in my ear. "Are you sure about that?" His fingers trace the mark on my neck, before traveling along the neckline of my dress to the curve of my breast.

"Yes."

"Hmm," he says pensively. "No."

"No?" I bite out.

"I think we should do it again." His lips return to my neck, his thumb brushing a tender nipple. "And again." Kiss. "And again."

Tilting my head back, I almost let it happen, almost let myself be swept away by his criminal mouth and his smoldering eyes. But no, I have a job. A dream job. Sort of.

I grab his forearms. "We can't." It sounds like a lie even to my ears. "We have to go."

He sighs but relents. "I'll let it go for now. But I mean it about that hickey." I flush. "And this conversation is not over. I will be in between your thighs again." He comes closer, "And you'll beg for more of my marks on your skin."

I swallow against the rush of arousal that sweeps my body at his words and nod shakily.

"Fine, we can discuss this later, but we have to leave now." I turn to the door. "And Danny?" I spin back towards him, bumping into the hard line of his body. "This never happened, okay?"

He smirks. "Whatever you say, freckles." He gives my ass a gentle tap.

I scowl at him and pull open the door. His laugh slides down my spine and I curse myself for ever being so foolish, because deep down I know he's right. This isn't going anywhere.

***

As soon as the car pulls up, Jess arrives on Danny's side of the car, handing him his sides for the day. Sarah accosts me before I can even close the door.

"What is the point of you if you can't even get him to set on time?"

Willing myself not to blush. I steel my spine ready to spit out any excuse that comes to mind when Danny says over the car, "My fault, I slept with my headphones in and didn't hear my alarm or the pounding on the door." He glances at me and adds, "Late night."

The blush deepens across my cheeks and I press my fingers to my nose awkwardly.

Luckily, Sarah doesn't notice. "No problem, we just swapped around you and Adriana. They're waiting for you now." She gestures to the makeup truck behind us.

Danny nods and turns to follow Jess. I go to follow him but Sarah's hand stops me.

"I'm not your boss but you need to step up. I know he's a liability but he's *your* liability."

I bite my tongue before I ask how I'm supposed to wake up Danny from his headphone sleep — his fake sleep — but Danny throws over his shoulder. "Anya, do you have my book?"

"Got to go," I mumble to Sarah before rounding the car to

where Danny is waiting, rummaging in my bag for the battered paperback I have carried around since I found him reading a thriller in his trailer. I pass it to him without looking in his eyes, a feat I have managed to accomplish since he last pierced my gaze in the bedroom mirror.

His fingers linger on mine as he takes the book, his skin brushing against my knuckles and sending a spark straight through my body. This was supposed to be gone, this energy between us. Worked out of our system by now.

I look at his Adam's apple, unwilling to look up any further.

"I'll uhm," I splutter, "I'll get you your coffee."

He nods, his tongue tracing his lips as if remembering my taste.

I glance up finally, looking into his eyes before ducking away to the catering truck.

I manage to successfully avoid him for the rest of the day, fetching him water and escorting him back and forth without so much as a word passing between us. Instead of hanging in his trailer, I lurk around the production truck under the guise of helping the production secretary, Sadie, organize transport.

At the end of the day, I get Danny in his car without so much as a word. He seems to have picked up on my 'don't acknowledge me' vibes so doesn't protest my silent treatment, though after wrap Jess has obviously picked up on the strange tension.

"Has he pissed you off or something? You guys are usually always whispering in the corner."

"Oh." I swallow, horrified that anyone has even picked that up. "I'm pissed at him for making us late this morning so I'm making him suffer."

"Love it, put him in his place." Jess laughs. "Is that a *hickey*?"

I slap a palm against my throat. "No I—uh— I burnt my hair on my straighteners," I laugh weakly.

"Oh, I've done that before," she winces in sympathy.

I say a quick goodbye before dashing past security and back into the city proper, walking instead of getting in the car with Danny. I'm tempted to hit up the local supermarket and grab a bottle of wine but decide I drank enough last night to last the whole month.

Finally on my own, I have the chance to sort through my muddled thoughts. This time yesterday Danny and I were getting closer, sharing life stories and a bottle of wine. Making terrible decisions. Although those terrible decisions felt gigantic when I was on set, in the dark of the night, last night doesn't feel so catastrophically awful.

Last night might have been…incredible.

It doesn't matter my personal feelings about the matter, I'm his paid assistant. Even if he didn't hire me, if people knew, I would garner the worst kind of reputation. My first job in the industry and I've already tried sleeping my way to the top. Even if it was unplanned, that's what everyone will say. No, it was good that we established this boundary now, before it got even more complicated.

We will act like nothing ever happened and everything will be fine.

Chapter 19

Anya is acting like nothing ever happened and it's driving me insane.

It's been days since I've had the best night of my life, since I felt her thick hair wrapped around my fist and tasted her soft mouth.

She's been doing her best to keep it professional, which is almost hilarious to watch as professional has never exactly been in Anya's repertoire. I almost think she's going to start ducking her head and calling me 'Sir'.

I wouldn't mind that actually.

I don't understand why she's being so weird about this. I know what we had was unlike anything I've ever experienced before. Not just the sex, but the whole day leading up to it. It was the first time I felt like myself, like I could be playful and joke, do anything to make her laugh.

I thought she felt it too, but this awkward formal Anya has me all twisted up.

She won't even come inside my trailer, instead deciding to stand outside like a five foot five bodyguard.

The only time I get to see her is when she ferries me from

base to set or the hotel. It's a unique kind of torture to sit so close to her and for her to barely even acknowledge me. Her head bent and buried in her phone, or speaking quiet French with Jaques.

I'm starting to doubt that that night had any effect on her, but I know in my soul that it's just a front she's putting on. It seems impossible that she can't feel anything when I can finally see a world in color that was sepia toned before.

Today, I'm shooting a court scene. Costume has fitted me with a three piece suit that's itchy yet silky at the same time. When I step out of the costume truck, Anya straightens from her guard post and I don't miss the double take she gives me. Nor do I miss the way her plump lips part as her eyes drop to my suit.

I can't stop the warmth that spreads through my body at her lustful gaze — there's no denying that I've caused a physical reaction in her. Thousands of women have reacted to me, I'd have to be blind to have not noticed them. But Anya's attention feels like the sun is beaming on me after years of rain.

As I come closer, I'm tempted to not stop until I have her pushed against the wall. On my approach, she shakes her head and forces a bland smile. "Ready?"

Irritation races through me. Why is she doing this? Why is she acting like we're complete strangers, when after the night we shared we are anything but?

My jaw clenches as I bite out, "Yep."

I turn and storm away, heading to the waiting car. I open the door with more force than necessary and instead of sliding across so she can jump in behind me, I sit. It's all I can do to not cross my arms across my chest like a child as I watch her slide in from the opposite side.

The car is silent apart from my huffing breaths. Anya doesn't notice, her head buried in that bloody phone.

"Here are your sides," she says, handing them without looking at me. I mumble a thanks, all too aware of what I'll say if I open my mouth much more.

My phone buzzes in my pocket. I'll have to hand it over to Anya before the scene starts shooting.

Pip: Are you on set today?

Me: Why?

Pip: Where is your base?

Me: Bois de Bologne

Pip: When are you on break? I'm in the mood for a set visit

"How long is the break between scenes?" I ask Anya without looking up.

"About two hours before the makeup chair but two and a half before turning," she says. Out of the corner of my eye, I can see her watching me. "Why?" I can tell her curiosity has gotten the better of her. I could be honest and say Pip might come and irritate me…or I could test her stubborn resolve a little.

After sending a text to Pip telling her to come, I power my phone off.

Glancing at her, I say vaguely, "I'll take my lunch in my trailer." I hand the phone to her, "Make it for two."

Her bottom lip falls as she takes my phone, her lips forming the perfect 'o' shape, reminding me of the last time I saw her mouth like that.

She seems to remember herself. "Why?" Her confusion mixing deliciously with what I have a strong feeling is jealousy. "For two?" She repeats dumbly.

"I'll have a visitor."

"A visitor?"

"I've already cleared it with Brian. It won't be a problem will it?"

Before Anya has a chance to reply, we pull up outside my trailer.

I bite back my burgeoning smirk as I climb out of the car, leaving Anya gaping in the back seat.

Chapter 20

The door closes behind him so quietly he might as well have slammed it.

I sit there, gaping like a fish for a few seconds before I scurry out the car after him. Who is he having lunch with? For a second, I thought he meant he wanted lunch for me too, so that we could eat together. Of course, that was stupid. He probably wants nothing to do with me. I need to stay away from him from now on. It's for the best. It's what I wanted to happen.

So why did my stomach ache at the thought?

I hurry behind him as he makes his way to set, clutching his dead phone in my hand. He never usually switches it off, usually trusting me to not be weird and look through it unless necessary. He doesn't want me to look at it at all. Is he already seeing someone else?

Not that what we had constituted *seeing* each other. Although, we definitely *saw* a lot of each other.

It was one night. It's no big deal, he's allowed to date whoever we wants.

Not that he's necessarily dating whoever he's invited to his trailer.

The set today is a courtroom, a local one in the fifteenth arrondissement. Danny immediately heads to Gwendoline, listening to her as she starts to block out the scene.

Spotting Lauren, I sidle up next to her.

"Hey," she says, not looking up from her iPad.

"Hey, do you know anything about a visitor for Danny today?"

She doesn't glance up. "Nope. Probably a French super-model or something to pass the time, you know how he is."

Lauren walks away after that lovely bombshell. A French supermodel. My chest burns and I have to physically unclench my jaw before I break a tooth.

The scene is a long one so I settle in the corridor outside the set, propped up against the wall with my arms crossed across my chest and Danny's switched off phone clutched in my fist. The scene rolls on and he's on fire. It's a tense scene, one where Danny's character has to defend himself with a quiet anger, keeping himself leashed. For once, Gwendoline has no notes for him, only the supporting actors or the camera angles.

Pride swells in my chest but I stomp it down. He's probably only doing well so he can get through the scene and burn off some energy in his trailer.

When they call wrap on the scene, I don't walk over to Danny and collect him like I usually do. I wait for him to come to me, the phone in my hand calling to him like a carrot on a stick. When he reaches me, I turn and walk away, his phone still in my hand.

Am I being petty? Yes. Do I care? No.

We get to the car and I open it for him. I feel his presence at my side as he holds his hand out expectantly. I drop his phone in his waiting palm.

"I'll stick around here. Jess has your lunch *orders*." I make sure to emphasize the plural. "I'll be back to pick you up for makeup in an hour and a half." I close the door behind him before biting through the open window. "Hope that's enough time for you."

I can't help the glare I level him with as he looks up and catches my eye for the first time in days. He gives me a saccharine grin. "Oh, it will be."

I give him a sarcastic smile that drops before he even looks away. I turn around, refusing to watch the car pull away. My insides boiling.

Later, after I've got enough strange looks from the crew for hanging around like a bad smell, I return to base.

My jaw hurts from how hard I've held it clenched. As I near the truck, I try to see if I can see it rocking. Logically, I know the structure is too sturdy but it wouldn't surprise me for Danny's thrusts to be that powerful.

Each step towards the truck feels like I'm walking through drying cement, the thought of his hands on another woman — a tall, beautiful woman who has probably never had a hair on her chin — makes me feel ready to throw up.

It's cruel really, to know what a night with Danny Covington is like. To know what his lips feel like on mine, and how his clever fingers can tease me to my peak. Even with the sour thoughts of what he's doing in his trailer, I can't stop the warm flush that envelopes my body at the memory of his lips tracing down my neck.

Taking a deep breath, I steel myself at the door to the trailer. *If he's going to be immature about this,* I think, *so will I.*

I bang on the door, loudly announcing my presence. I yank it open with a level of force that almost knocks me back down the narrow steps, and I raise my hand to cover my eyes — partially for self preservation but mostly for the drama.

"You're needed in makeup," I snap into the darkness.

My senses are heightened. The door slams behind me and I listen out for any noises from the direction of the couch. Nothing. My imagination runs wild. Maybe they haven't moved at all, maybe he's still deep in the throes. Is that a rustle? Is that him or her? Is he pulling his clothes back on?

"What are you doing?" Danny asks with an amused lilt. I don't have to look at him to know he's smirking. Prick.

"I don't want to burn my retinas," I say primly.

He chuckles softly, I swear I feel his breath on my face. When did he get so close?

"Put your hand down, freckles."

Biting my cheek and preparing myself to look at his conquest, I lower my hand, pinning him with my coldest glare.

Out of the corner of my eye, I scan the trailer.

We're alone.

"What did you think I was doing in here?"

He looks the same as he did when I left him, dark t-shirt perfectly sculpted to his chest and a heated look in his eye. I cross my arms across my chest. "Just wanted to give you your privacy."

"That's a first."

I huff, hands falling to my sides.

"My sister dropped by an hour ago."

I blink. "Your sister?"

"Flying visit before meeting friends in the Marais." His smile is cocky. "Did you think I had someone in here, freckles?"

Refusing to meet his gaze, I step back. He follows me moving into my space until my back is against the counter.

"Did you think I had a woman in here?" His hands rest on the counter, caging me in. His proximity makes me instantly woozy, and my legs start to wobble. His piercing eyes drop to my mouth.

"You did have a woman in here," I protest, weakly. His proximity is overwhelming. If he tilts forward just slightly we'll be kissing.

"Freckles."

I swallow. "You need to be in makeup."

"Not yet." He tilts his head forward slightly until his forehead rests against mine. I couldn't move away even if I wanted to. My heart is beating so loud I'm sure he can hear it. "Come on baby, tell me. Tell me what you think I was doing in this trailer."

Tingles erupt across my body as his breath fans my cheek.

"I thought—" I break off, my mouth dry. Curse him for doing this to me.

"Did you think I was fucking someone else? While you were on the other side of the door torturing yourself with the thought?"

He presses closer to my body, my breasts brushing against his chest with every haggard breath I inhale. As he presses closer, words and anger escape me in a breath that brushes against his cheeks. All that is left is the feel of him pressed against me and the sound of my thumping heart.

"There's only one woman I want." This is torture. He tilts my chin with his fingers, dragging my eyes to him. My eyelids feel heavy and arousal takes control of my body, as easy as breathing. "You want that too, don't you baby?"

His lips ever so slightly brush mine. I hear a whimper and with a jolt realize it came from me.

His lips pull away, and my head feels like it's attached to a magnet as I chase him in his retreat. I'm going to explode if he doesn't touch me. Suspended in the moment, all I can think about it the feel of his lips on mine. Anticipation thrums in my chest.

Ignoring the small voice in the back of my head that's telling me this is a terrible idea, I capture his lips with mine.

Pulling back, lips tingling, I finally look in his eyes. And then we explode.

He crushes into me. My hands raise to his head, tangling in his hair and pulling him closer. His arms tighten around my waist before he effortlessly lifts me onto the counter.

His weight between my spread legs makes me moan as I feel his hardness right *there.*

He grinds into me, biting my bottom lip before his fingers come to my chin, clasping it tightly and forcing me to look up at him. His thumb pulls at my bottom lip, opening my mouth wider.

"You've been ignoring me." His eyes are glued to my plump lip under his fingertip. "Tell me you feel this Anya." He rubs his nose against mine. "Tell me you want this as much as I do. Tell me this distance has been driving you crazy."

I can't remember how to speak. I whimper as his other hand spreads up my leg, moving to the juncture between my thighs. His fingers tease the seam of my jeans and my eyes flutter closed.

"Tell me baby, and I'll give you what you want."

Heart pounding, I'm desperate to clamp my thighs together, to make his fingers move and relieve this torturous ache.

"Please," I beg. "I want you." He groans and presses his fingers firmly though my jeans.

"You're mine, Anya." He tilts my head back, that damn thumb pulling my mouth open wider. My heart races as I somehow know exactly what he's going to do. He brushes his thumb against my lip, and my mouth follows it, my toes curling in my shoes. His thumb scrapes across my bottom teeth and my tongue flicks against his skin. I open wider for him, wrapping my lips around his digit, desperate to be feel him on my tongue.

With a groan, he yanks his hand away and replaces it with his mouth. We attack each other with frenzy. I clamp my legs around his hips, pulling him closer, his length pressing against me, in the most delicious tease. He quickly unbuttons my jeans and plunges his fingers into my underwear, his attention right where I need him. I let out a haggard breath as I desperately reach for his zipper, taking his cock in my hand.

"Condom?" I ask breathlessly, as I squeeze his hot length.

He pulls my jeans off completely, throwing them on the floor and reaching into his pocket. He hands me a condom and I take over, rolling it over him as an excuse to touch him. I guide him to me and the first flex of his hips has him sliding into me. Deep.

We both freeze at the sensation. His head buries into my neck as he groans. I clutch his hair and try to catch my breath. He rolls his hips, pulling out and back in so, so slowly. His hands settle on my ass, pulling me onto him in time with each flex of his hips.

His fingers return to my clit, and it isn't long before I'm tumbling off the edge, his tongue in my mouth, his fingers on my clit and his cock deep inside me.

He follows soon after, clutching my thighs tightly to his hips.

I rest my forehead against his chest, still covered by his t-shirt. I can feel his heart beating erratically through the cotton.

God, we didn't even take all our clothes off. He presses a kiss to my forehead and slowly pulls out.

"Danny," I start softly. I don't even know how I'm going to finish my sentence.

He brushes the hair out of my face and tilts my head gently to look at him. "Don't. Don't deny us this."

I take a deep breath, his blue eyes pleading. Maybe it's the orgasm but I can't think of a single reason not to do this. Not to allow myself — us — this electric chemistry.

Whatever he sees in my eyes has him backing off, reaching for my jeans and helping me hop off the counter. Which is good because my legs are trembling so much I don't think I can stand.

"I'm going to freshen up," I say, clutching my jeans to my chest and heading for the small bathroom.

"Okay."

Closing the door behind me, I race to the sink and splash cool water on my face. Looking in the mirror, I take in my bedraggled appearance. I look like I've been thoroughly fucked. Great.

Pulling my jeans back on and attempting to look respectable, I take a steadying breath and head back into the room.

He's where I left him, leaning against the counter. My tongue feels heavy in my mouth.

"Okay look freckles, before you say anything, you need to stop overthinking it." He runs his hand through his hair. "This doesn't have to be anything more than it is."

I swallow. "I just need some time."

"Let's talk after wrap."

I nod shakily, still trying to lower my blood pressure.

He nods seriously. "That was pretty hot though."

An incredulous laugh bubbles out of me. Trust him to make me laugh at a time like this.

"I'll come back to take you to makeup soon," I say as I push the door open, rushing down the stairs into the fresh air as I try to decide what the hell I'm going to say after wrap.

Chapter 21

ANYA

The last scene of the day is in the courtroom again, which means I can't linger near the action and have to wait in the hallway. Despite being near the craft table, it feels like I'm waiting for a sentencing myself.

I spend the entire scene leaning up against the wall, avoiding eye contact with any of the crew lest they can somehow tell what I've been up to in Danny's trailer. The stubborn flush in my cheeks is relentless, hardly fading as the memories of his hands on my body serve as a wicked reminder.

I pull out my phone for something to do, scrolling mindlessly through emails, desperately trying to assemble my jumbled thoughts into some sort of order.

Could I really jeopardize my career by sleeping with the lead star?

With *Danny Covington*?

Would everyone know? There is no way it wouldn't spread like wildfire if it got out. People would roll their eyes at Danny sleeping with someone who is essentially his PA, but me? I would be branded a slut and probably blacklisted for the rest of my career, destroying it before it even began.

Would he even want to do it again? Now that we've done it twice, maybe he's over it. Maybe he's got it–me–out of his system. Which would be a good thing. Obviously. Even if I would probably sell my kidney just to bury my head in his chest and feel his strong arms wrap around me one more time.

I could survive on just the memories, and one day when my grandchildren are watching *Better You Know* on TV, I can point and say *"He was a fabulous lover."* and cackle whilst they all cringe. I could cope with that.

Of course, that would mean I would have to deal with seeing him everyday for the next month, knowing exactly what he tastes like and the look on his face when he comes.

What could he possibly want to talk about? Surely he'll just say that it will never happen again. Why would Danny Covington want to keep hooking up with *me*? There are plenty of other women who would be happy and willing to warm his bed. Or his trailer. God, I bite my lip and glance around the empty hallway as memories of this afternoon assault me. Maybe he only wants me because I'm here. Because I'm convenient.

I cannot sleep with him again and ruin my career. I just can't! My job isn't even a real job for god's sake, and I need to nurture as many connections and get as much experience as I can possibly squeeze out of this position. Sleeping with Danny Covington would only make that infinitely more complicated. Even if it is the best sex of my life.

"That's a wrap, great work everyone." I hear Rachel shout from the set. I stand straight and decide that whatever Danny has to say to me now, I will leave with my dignity and my clothing intact.

Danny slides out of the room, glancing around until he spots me. I take a calming breath and head over to him. I pull his phone out of my pocket and hand it to him.

"Good scene?" I ask, awkwardly.

He nods, placing his phone in his pocket without powering it on. "Yeah." He licks his lip and I pull my hand to flatten nonexistent wayward strands of my hair.

"Let's go," I say. "Costume are de-rigging you here so you can just go straight home."

He nods and follows me to the room allocated by costume so he can change into his street clothes.

I wait outside, trying really hard not to think about the fact that a wooden door is all that separates me from his naked body.

He emerges fully dressed in jeans and a t-shirt and I nearly swallow my tongue. How is he so gorgeous? And how have I already had him? Twice!

We leave, waving goodbye to people as we pass. I don't look at him, even when we settle in the car. I find myself pressing against the door, as if to increase the limited space between us. Will he say something now? I hear him breathe and can feel his gaze on the side of my face.

I practically dislocate my neck peering out the window.

We pull up outside his hotel.

"Freckles," he says softly.

With a glance at Jaques, I turn to him, a false smile pulling at my lips. "You must be tired, it's been a long day."

"Yeah, it's been an eventful day." His eyes burn into mine for a heated second before he gets out and rounds to my side. My hand lingers on the door. When I open it, something is going to happen. If I stay right here, nothing will be said and everything will stay the same. I catch Jaques' quirked eyebrow in the rear-view mirror and the distraction allows Danny to pull my door open.

I gulp. Saying a fumbling goodbye to Jaques, I clamber out of the car. I rub my sweaty palms on my jeans and I wait until the car pulls away from the curb before I say, "Well I should get goin—"

"Freckles," he interrupts, grabbing my fingers. Before I have time to speak, he's pulling me through the front doors.

Dutifully, I follow him through the lobby, marveling at the feel of his warm palm in mine. The foyer is empty as we make our way to the elevator.

Before the doors even finish closing he's on me, pressing me into the wall as his lips descend on mine. I moan as I part my lips for him, my hands rising to the nape of his neck.

His body presses into mine as he groans, his lips leaving mine to run down my neck, licking and kissing as he explores my skin.

"Danny," I breathe, as his lips catch mine again. "We said we'd talk."

"We will." He says against my lips. "After."

The elevator doors opening save me from speaking. He pulls away and tugs me into the hallway. Anything I had planned to say earlier has slipped between my fingers like the strands of his smooth hair. When he releases me to pull his key from his pocket, I press my fingers to my tingling lips.

Get it together Anya, I tell myself.

Inside the room, he presses me against the door, claiming my lips again, his tongue teasing mine. I can't catch my breath, let alone summon the words that are lingering at the edge of my mind.

"You taste so fucking good," he mumbles as he runs his hands down my side, clasping my thigh in his hand and hiking it around his hip. I whimper at the new angle as he grinds into me.

Heat spreads across my body at the pressure. My hands work their way back to his hair, my fingers spreading through the silky strands. I tug his hair until his head pulls back. His hooded eyes linger on my surely swollen lips.

I swallow. "We need to talk."

We both take a breath, my chest heaving, brushing against his.

He steps back and readjusts himself in his jeans. "Do you, ah, want a drink? I have wine."

"God, yes." I pull the hair off my neck, attempting to cool down. "Wait, no. Wine and *this*," I wave my hand between us, "is a terrible hindrance on my ability to think logically."

He smirks as he hands me a glass. "I already poured."

I take it gratefully, swallowing a large swig as I perch on the small armchair.

He sits on the coffee table, so close to me his knees on either side of mine. He sets his glass on the table.

"So," he says, looking entirely too pleased at my flustered bumbling.

"So," I parrot, taking another gulp. "You go first."

He laughs as he runs his hands through his hair, "I think you know what I'm going to say."

I shake my head. I have no idea what's going through his head.

"I like fucking you." Well then. "And I think you like it too. So we should do it again."

I can't help the laugh that bubbles out of me. "It's pretty simple when you say it like that."

His grin lights me up inside.

I take another sip of my wine, the whole glass nearly empty.

"Do you?" he asks, his blue eyes dark.

"Stop looking at me like that and saying things to me."

He laughs, "So don't look at you or speak to you?"

"Ideally."

"Sure thing." He doesn't look away.

Taking a deep breath, I try to assemble my thoughts. "Okay, so I mean. You are — you. Ah, I don't know!"

"Why are you overthinking this, freckles?"

"I'm not *over*thinking, I'm just *thinking*."

He stays silent, his fingers tracing my thigh through my jeans.

"If anything, I'm doing your thinking for you," I say.

"I'm usually pretty good at doing that on my own, but thank you."

"So," I pause. "You want to…"

"Fuck you, yes."

"Gah." I stand and escape to the window.

He follows, his hand coming to rest on my hip.

"What is it baby? If you don't want this, it's okay." His hand drifts to my front, his pinky finger resting on the slip of skin where my shirt has ridden up. "But I think you do want this." I place my hand on the window. We're high up enough that the people on the street can't see us but it doesn't stop the streak of arousal that pools in my belly.

He gently brushes my hair over my shoulder and I can't help but tilt my head, baring my neck to him. His hot mouth presses a kiss against my pulse and his wicked fingers open the button of my jeans.

My head falls back against his chest as his hand descends

into my underwear, his fingers finding the evidence of my arousal instantly. His finger strokes gently teases my clit and I moan. Am I really letting this happen?

I can just about make out our reflection in the window. The sight of his lips on my throat, his strong arm banded across my chest and his hands in my jeans, is almost enough to send me over the edge.

"Tell me what you want, baby," he says, nipping my ear with his teeth.

There's no use denying what my body is screaming. "I want you," I admit with a whisper.

I protest as he pulls his hand out of my jeans and spins me so my back is pressing against the cool glass of the window. His mouth finally claims mine. His tongue licks across my bottom lip as I open for him.

"Say it again."

"I want you."

His hands tighten on my hips as he twists me again, walking me back until I fall on the mattress. My hands make quick work of his belt until I'm tugging his cock free. He groans as I wrap my hand around him, pumping him once, twice. He yanks my jeans down my legs and I laugh as they get stuck on my shoes.

He quickly throws my clothes across the room. He grabs a condom from the bedside table and comes to rest between my spread legs.

"Yeah?" He asks, breathlessly, holding his cock at the base.

I lick my lips. I think I might die if I don't feel him inside me. "Please," I beg, reaching for him.

He hitches himself at my entrance and with the softest kiss, pushes inside me. I moan at the sensation, his hardness filling me and hitting that spot deep inside me. He thrusts, gently at first before speeding up. My whole body moves at the force of his movements and my hand stretches to the headboard for support. He leans up on his arm and his hand descends between us. I cry at the first brush of his fingers on my clit and it isn't long before I'm falling off the edge, my orgasm barreling through me in waves and waves of pleasure.

Danny doesn't give me a moment to recover before his hand slides beneath my thigh and pulls my leg to my chest. The new angle sends sparks through my body.

"Freckles," he groans before his orgasm overtakes him and he collapses on top of me, burying his head in my neck.

We lie there as we catch our breath, his weight on top of me the most comforting embrace. Eventually, pressing a kiss to my lips, he rolls off me, disposing of the condom before opening his arm to me. I rest my head on his chest and run my fingers across his toned abdomen.

He kisses my hair, his fingers playing with the strands.

"So," he says, "are we doing this?"

I rest my chin on his chest as I look up at him.

"What is this?" I ask, curious as to what he's going to say.

He throws me that wicked smirk. "We can figure that out along the way. But for now, we hang out, we fuck, we enjoy ourselves."

It sounds like the worst idea I've ever had. Maybe my orgasm has rattled my brain but I still can't quite deny myself this. We can be discreet, can't we?

"Okay," I say.

His smile is almost blinding. "Okay."

I rest my head back on his chest, listening to his heart beat.

"We'll need to keep this quiet."

I snort. "Obviously. I'm not having everyone on set thinking I'm trying to get a leg up."

He chuckles as he rolls so I'm underneath him, he swipes his nose across mine. "Let's keep it just between us."

"Just us," I agree as his lips claim mine once more.

Chapter 22

DANNY

There is no other way I want to wake up. With Anya's smooth leg slung over my hip and her hair tickling my nose as she buries her head in my neck. My limbs are stiff from the position I have refused to move from all night and the rounds we went through before collapsing out of sheer exhaustion.

I play with the ends of her hair and breathe her in. Soon she starts to stir, her breathy moan as she wakes immediately sending blood rushing to my cock. I rest my palm on her thigh, pulling her tighter into me.

She blinks up at me with sleepy eyes.

"Morning," I say, unable to stop myself from pressing a kiss to her nose.

"Hello," she says softly, so different from the frantic evacuation the last time we woke up together.

"What time is it?"

"Just gone seven."

She takes a breath and detangles her limbs from mine. My heart drops at the thought of her leaving the bed but she turns onto her side, pulling me by the forearm. I let her manhandle me until she is curled on her side and I'm curved around her back. I don't stop myself from grinding into her ass and pressing a kiss to her neck. I'm delighted when I'm rewarded with another breathy moan for my efforts.

She arches her back, pressing her ass into my groin. My hands wander along her skin until I cup her breast, my fingertip grazing her hardened nipple. I'm half expecting her to stop me, for her to tell me we haven't got time but she opens her legs, hooking one over my thigh. Taking the invitation, my hand travels down her smooth stomach. My fingers trace the outline of her underwear, sliding under the elastic.

Her phone buzzes on the nightstand, freezing both of us in our tracks and dissolving the moment into the air. I rest my head on her shoulder and try to control my erection.

She pulls her legs back together and reaches for her phone, curving her back in a way she must realize drives me wild.

Anya flops onto her back with a yawn as she checks her phone. I rise on my elbow as I study her sleepy face. She rubs her eye and says, "I need to go back to my place and get changed."

"Okay." Neither of us move. She turns her head into my chest and presses a kiss to my skin.

"I think I'll just meet you on set, just to assuage any suspicion."

"I don't think anyone will have any suspicions, freckles."

"Better safe than sorry," she says as she leans into me. It's the easiest thing in the world to press my lips to hers.

She squirms against my mouth. "Morning breath."

I ignore her and open wider for her, the hint of her tongue forcing me to push her back against the mattress, hands wandering.

"Get it out of your system now," she says, pulling away.

"We're not doing this on set again."

"Not even to repeat what happened yesterday?"

By now, I think I would have fucked the blush out of her but she loves to surprise me. Pink splotches appear on her cheeks, telling me exactly how she feels about our impromptu session.

Her fingers come between our mouths, as if she needs to physically peel herself off me.

"We'll only meet at the hotel then," I say, placatingly.

"What if people see me coming and going?"

"People have already seen you coming and going." I flop down beside her, clasping her hand in mine and playing with her fingers. "Usually dragging me out by the ear."

Anya scoffs and gives me what I will now and forever call a 'loving tap'.

"We should mix it up. Keep them on their toes."

"Who is 'them'?" I laugh.

"Shut up." She bites her lip. "You can come to mine sometimes."

My smile pulls at my cheek. "You're so cute when you get shy."

"I'm not shy." She gives me a shove. "You don't have to come to the apartment, gosh."

I raise my arm and squeeze her to me. "I want to come to your place, Anya."

I kiss her forehead.

She eventually pulls away from me and picks up her clothes. "I'll go home and get changed, and I'll meet you at work. Can you get there okay without me?"

"Can I go downstairs and get in the car without you?" I sit up, resting my arms on my bent knee. "I think I can manage, freckles."

"Very funny." Anya pulls her shoes on before she leans down and presses a final kiss to my mouth before heading out the door. I get a vision of the future, her coming to kiss me goodbye every morning before she leaves. I shake it off. Just yesterday we agreed we would keep it casual, see where it goes. It's way too soon to be imagining a future of lazy mornings and goodbye kisses.

But as the door closes behind her, I can't stop the grin that pulls at my mouth.

***

There is nothing that could happen today that would ruin my good mood. I finally got the girl I can't get out of my mind, into my bed, with an understanding that she would return. I try to contort my face into my regular blasé expression and not the dopey grin I know I currently have.

Anya's waiting for me when I step out of the car a few hours later, handing me my sides and a coffee. If I let my fingers linger on hers when I take the cup out of her hand, that's our business.

I watch her bite the corner of her plump lip as she breaks our connection. "Straight to makeup today."

"No down time?" I throw her a cheeky grin.

She narrows her eyes at me. "Not today." We fall into step as we head to the makeup trailer. "You can have some *time* after wrap. Back at your hotel." It's adorable that she thinks her little code is subtle.

I throw her an incredibly subtle wink in return. She rushes to open the door to the trailer ahead of me. I hold the door open over her head and usher her inside. Keeping things low-key is one thing but my girl being my personal doorman makes the gentleman inside me wince.

We step into the makeup truck and my good mood plummets like a lead balloon.

Sat in the chair next to mine, a white makeup bib around his neck, is Callum McBride. He looks over at me and greets me with an overly enthusiastic,"There he is. The leading man."

My teeth clench together and I am frozen to the spot. I feel Anya's hand flutter at my back giving me a gentle nudge to move.

Sally gestures for me to sit in the chair next to McBride. I stare straight ahead. Unfortunately, that requires me looking at my own face. I would much rather see the dopey grin I've had since this morning than the dark scowl I currently can't budge. Refusing to let my eyes flicker to McBride, I instead fix my gaze on Anya who warily leans against the opposite wall. I know her tension is due to the blond asshole sat next to me, currently charming the artist who is attaching his ridiculous fake beard to his jaw.

Still, the sight of her relaxes me into my seat.

"Haven't seen you around much Daniel. Not like you, party boy, eh?" McBride goads.

I take a deep breath. "I have better things to do with my time than sniff coke with you, Callum."

McBride bleats a laugh. "Since when?"

My teeth grind together. Anya steps forward and unfurls my fingers. To my surprise, I let her drop my wireless headphones in my hand. I glance up at her but she ignores me and heads back to the wall.

"May I?" I ask Sally, gesturing to the headphones.

"Go for it," Sally replies, focusing on mixing her various potions.

I place the headphones in my ears, effectively stopping any other attempts by McBride to distract me. I quickly realize Anya has my phone. I look up at her and watch as she connects to my headphones and immediately Leon Bridges plays in my ears.

I huff a laugh and run my fingers across my mouth to hide the smile. God, she's amazing. She's given me a way to ignore McBride whilst distracting me from my irritation. I let the music play in my ears, ignoring the man next to me and resting my eyes on the only person in the room who understands exactly what I need.

***

I should have known my good day wasn't to last. Despite Anya's intervention in the truck, McBride has already pledged to make my life as difficult as possible. Today, I haven't made it easy for him. I've ignored every incessant attempt to trip me up during a scene. I've kept a cool head.

It's when we're getting our mics taken off that he strikes.

"Like the hotel?" he asks, innocently.

I ignore him.

"Those suites are pretty nice," McBride continues.

My shoulders tense. "What floor are you on?" I ask pleasantly.

"Seven."

Two floors below me. I relax knowing that the prospect of him seeing Anya coming and going is pretty slim. Unless he sees her in the lobby. No, even if he did see her it would just look like she's coming to get me for a work related reason, so unless she emerges with sex hair and rumpled clothes, we'll be fine. Anya's concern from this morning suddenly becomes a little more worrisome. Maybe we do need to switch up our

151

schedules.

McBride is prattling on in my ear but I've got what I need from him. Patting the sound guy on the shoulder in thanks when he releases me, I walk away.

Anya is waiting by the car, her nose buried in her phone. She looks up as I approach, her face brightening with a smile that almost takes my breath away.

"Good day?" she asks, straightening.

I reach around her, crowding her against the car. "Yeah."

Her eyes drop to my mouth, her pink tongue flicking against her lip. Teasing Anya is quickly becoming my favorite part of the day. I open the door and gesture for her to enter.

Once we're on the move, Anya glances at Jaques before turning to face me. "Did the hotel speak to you about the linen?"

I'm confused for a second until I register her *just to go with it* expression. "*Oh*, no?" I ask, innocently.

She nods. "I'll come and speak to them for you."

Ah. "Yes, I really need my linen seen to. My whole bed actually, definitely needs a work over."

She rolls her eyes but she can't hide the grin on her face from me.

After saying a quick goodbye to Jaques, we bypass the lobby and any hotel staff who probably could advise on bed linen, heading straight to the elevators.

I take her hand in mine as soon as the doors close, tugging her into my space. She leans in expectantly, but I quickly relay my McBride woes.

"Oh," Anya tries to take a step away from me but I pull her back into my arms.

"He's not in the elevator with us freckles, we're fine. It's the communal areas we need to be wary of. No fondling me in reception."

She snorts a laugh and presses a kiss to my lips. I chase her as she pulls away, the ping of the door forcing me to drop her hand.

Chapter 23

ANYA

The next day is a rest day and Danny has been busy with long hours everyday. This week has been mostly lengthy, intense scenes and I can tell most of the cast and crew have been a little bit stunned by the effort he's putting in. I'm not. I knew he just needed a push, a little support.

And regular orgasms.

Although, they haven't been too regular with our busy schedules, the not-on-set rule I created, and the not-in-public rule he made. Options have been significantly limited. There are really only so many excuses I can make to go up to follow him up to his room when Jaques drops him off.

That's why, after a late wrap last night, I suggested we could meet at my place today. Danny's answering groan of relief was all I needed. "Do you have a regular sized fridge?"

So here I am, frantically cleaning the entire apartment. My phone rings in my pocket. I pull my rubber gloves off and tuck my phone between my shoulder and ear.

"I'm lost," Danny huffs into the phone before I say a word.

"You really do need to be handheld at all times, don't you?" I throw the gloves and cleaning products under the sink.

"I would be fine if your instructions weren't 'big door on the right'."

"What can you see?"

"Lots of big fucking doors on the right."

I laugh and open the window on the Juliet balcony. Leaning over the railing, I spot Danny up the street with one hand on his phone and the other on his hip.

"Now tell me," I say cheekily. "Can you tell your left from your right?."

"I came from a different direction!"

I lean further out the window and stick my fingers in my mouth, letting out a wolf whistle. Danny spins in my direction and I can see his glare from here. I wave.

"You better hope no one else heard that," he says, crossing the street to my door.

"I think you'll live. I'll buzz you up. Fourth floor."

Once I confirm he's in the building, I anxiously start fluffing pillows as I wait. How long does it take him to walk up four flights of stairs for god's sake? I'm trying really hard not to think about how this is the first time that we've met up somewhere other than his hotel, that this is the first time that we've arranged to meet up outside of work.

A light knock sounds at the door, making me jump.

"Who is it?" I tease.

"Noise complaint. Something about a whistle."

I swing the door open and try not to swallow my tongue at the sight of his bright blue eyes.

"You going to let me in?"

God, I'm just standing still staring at him like a fool. "Uh, yeah." I step back and he moves. I freeze. This is so not like normal. Should I kiss him? Hug him? High five?

"Stop being weird, freckles." He looks around my apartment pensively. He pokes his head into every room and I follow along, awkwardly hovering over his shoulder.

"I'm not being weird." Should I give him a tour? Or just show him the way to the bedroom?

He finally settles his attention on me, his lips rising in his insufferable smirk.

"Is this place a rental?"

Huh? "No, it's my Aunt's. She's traveling."

That smirk grows. "Anya, this place is posh."

I bristle. "No it's not."

"Anya," he says slowly, placing his hands on my shoulders. "You're posh."

I gasp and shrug his arms off. "Take that back!"

"God, all those comments about my fancy hotel and my sushi preferences and you're hiding this in the back pocket."

"I am not posh," I bite.

"You're a little Champagne Socialist, that's what you are." He taps my nose and brushes past me through to the living room.

I follow him and watch as he settles on my couch. I try really hard not to recognize how at home he looks there, how he would look sprawled there every day.

"Want a drink?" I peel my eyes away from him before my mind runs too far away.

"Don't worry," he looks around. "The butler will be here shortly."

I throw one of my freshly plumped pillows at him as he laughs, but before I can get in a second swing, he grabs my arm and tugs me towards him.

I collapse onto him and his hands clutch my waist as he

presses his lips to mine. He swallows my moan as his tongue teases me.

My hands find his hair and tug, until he's leaning against the cushions and I'm straddling his lap. He kisses his way down my neck, the hands under my ass grinding me against him. My breath hitches as the bulge beneath his jeans hits just the right spot.

In a smooth motion, he grasps my thighs and twists us so I'm underneath him and his delicious weight squishes me. His lips return to my neck, his tongue licking at my skin like a live wire igniting my blood.

His hand wanders up my shirt and he groans into my mouth when he discovers the bare skin underneath. A good decision to forgo the bra I guess. He tugs my shirt off, exposing my peaked nipples to the cool air. His fingers flick over my nipple and he squeezes my breast in his hand, following the movement with his mouth. He travels down my body, kissing and licking my skin until he nestles between the cradle of my thighs.

My heart pounds in my ears as he unbuttons my jeans. He gives me space to pull them off and fling them across the room. He rips his t-shirt over his head, allowing my hands to roam across his torso, tangling my fingers in his dark chest hair. A small voice in my head reminds me to consider how I look, to contort my body so there are no rolls on my belly, but the wet kiss he presses to my inner thigh distracts me. His strong hands grip the outside of each thigh and wrench them further apart. His nose brushes against my folds and he presses a light kiss to the bundle of nerves begging for attention.

"Fuck, Anya," he groans. "You're so wet. Have you been like this all day baby, waiting for me?" He kisses the crease of my thigh and looks up at me with hooded eyes.

"No," I lie, my eyes fluttering closed. A sharp bite on my inner thigh has them flying open again and a shudder runs down my spine.

"Liar," he returns his attention to my parted thighs. "I bet you've been thinking about this all day." His breath brushes against me, making my breath catch in my throat. "Been thinking about my cock all day haven't you, freckles?"

I can't take it anymore. "Yes," I whimper. "Please."

"Because you asked so nicely." His tongue swipes with a strong lick and my back arches off the couch. Danny consumes me with a frenzy, licking and sucking and kissing. He lifts my hips off the cushion and closer to his mouth, like he could swallow me whole.

I watch as his breathing grows frantic and his eyes flick up to mine. His smoldering gaze combined with his wicked tongue sends me careening over the edge.

I catch my breath and he releases me with a final kiss to my sensitive flesh, lowering me back onto the couch.

He falls forward and presses his lips to mine. Before, with other men, I would have turned away before they kissed me, but with Danny I chase his lips as he pulls away, desperate for another taste. He kisses my cheek gently before lying between my open legs, his head resting on my heaving chest.

My eyes close as the comforting weight of his body and the affect of my orgasm almost lulls me to sleep.

"I can hear your heart," he says softly.

"Hmm?" I murmur, not quite back on Earth.

"Yeah, it's saying 'Danny-gives-the-best-head.'"

I laugh and flick his cheek. "Don't call it head."

"What am I supposed to call it? Licking the bean?"

I grimace, "It's called cunnilingus."

"Doesn't roll off the tongue as easily as rug munching," he quips.

"Ew!" I squeal and try to push him upright. He laughs and lets his body become dead weight, so I dig into his sides in retaliation. We battle until he nearly rolls off the couch and calls a ceasefire. We collapse again with flushed faces and racing hearts.

His head resumes its position against my chest. I could push him off for real and put some clothes on, but I can't think of a single reason why. My fingers push through his hair, lightly scratching with my nails. It's so quiet, I think he's fallen asleep. What man comes to a woman's house, eats her out and then falls asleep? Who did I blow in a past life to deserve this?

"Anya," Danny mumbles. Not asleep then.

"Yeah?"

"I think the butler forgot my drink order."

My groan dissolves into a laugh as he raises his head to look at me, a silly grin on his face and his hair wild from my hands. "You're insufferable."

"And yet you suffer me." He presses a kiss to my lips. "Drink now, please."

I roll my eyes, but can't help my smile as I push at his shoulders. "Get off me, you big brute."

He eases off me and I grab his discarded t-shirt before heading to the kitchen. By the time I return with a glass of water, Danny has pulled his jeans back on and is inspecting the room, admiring the trinkets acquired from Claudette's many travels.

The room is light and airy with chic, practical furniture, but dotted around the room is an assortment of gemstones, figurines, and general tat that Sabine would never allow to clutter up her house. The two bed terraced house I grew up in feels miles away from this luxurious Parisian apartment.

"It's my aunt's place, Claudette." I explain. "She's rolling in money – I don't know why, and I haven't asked, but mum and I are just regular people."

"Your aunt lives here full time?"

"She has a house in the south and a chalet in Switzerland. She doesn't even rent this place out."

"She's letting you rent though."

"Yeah, it's a whole thing." I wave my hand. "I think she just likes being useful so she can hold it over my mum's head. I don't have any siblings, so I don't really get it."

"I could tell you were an only child." He nudges me. "So bossy."

I roll my eyes. "You have a sister, right?"

"Younger, Pip. We used to be at each other's throats all the time." He picks up a figurine. "We were more like strangers than siblings, because we were always away working or at school. And then when we were together, our parents would just be comparing us to each other – our careers and what we were doing next. It took years for us to realize that it wasn't me against her, but us against them."

"So you're close now?"

"We make an effort. I stayed with her earlier this year in LA but then I had to move to France," he looks at me wily. "She's coming over again for a collab with a fashion house soon so you'll probably see her around."

I bite down on the twist in my belly. Meeting his sister?

As if Danny knew where my head was at, he says, "She mentioned coming to set, so."

An awkward silence commences. Our arrangement works when it's just the two of us in my apartment or his hotel room, but then the outside world comes knocking and douses us with cold water.

Danny's hand lingers on Claudette's beat-up guitar resting in the corner of the room. His fingers trace the strings, plucking a discordant twang. Before I can ask if he plays, he picks up a photo frame. The photo is dated and old. "Is this your mum?" he asks.

I take a closer look. "Yeah that's her."

In the photo, Sabine dances with her brown hair curled in an 80s wave, holding the hand of Claudette, who is bent in half with laughter.

"You look like her." Danny says.

"Yeah, we get that a lot."

"You miss her," he says.

"I talk to her most days but it's still not enough sometimes."

"Where is home?" Danny asks, like he can't believe he doesn't know.

"A small village with about a thousand people and a pub. The people who live there have always lived there. I moved out after uni but go back as often as I can to see people. What about you? You grew up in London?"

"Mostly. We moved around a lot so it was a base of sorts. But as soon as *Better You Know* kicked off, I left school and had on set tutors. So I didn't have, like, school friends or anything, no one I keep in touch with."

"Wait, so you don't have all the people from school on Facebook?" I ask, puzzled.

He shakes his head.

"But how do you keep up with who's gotten married or

started fights in the pub or named their babies something stupid like Hawk?"

Danny snorts. "Hawk?"

"There are two from my year alone."

"You have to be famous and audacious to get away with that."

I laugh. "Please name your future child something like 'Candle'."

Danny chuckles, "Nah, I'm more partial to a food themed name. Broccoli."

"Parmesan."

"Lasagna."

"This is an Italian child of course."

"Well, obviously."

I stop my snort escaping with a hand to my mouth.

"You have a beautiful laugh," he says.

I chuckle. "Shut up."

Danny reaches out with his finger and brushes it along my temple, pushing my hair off my face. "I should probably go," he says.

I clear my throat. "Yeah of course. Well thanks for the…" I wave my hand.

"The orgasm?" he asks.

"Yeah, that." My cheeks burn.

He grins and steps into my space. He cradles my face and lowers his lips to mine. I melt into his kiss and whine as he releases me, looking into my eyes. "I'm going to need my shirt back."

Ignoring the sinking feeling in my chest at the thought of him leaving, I whip it off without looking at him. What am I doing? This is a casual hookup. I shouldn't expect him to stay.

I cover my body the best I can as I pull my clothes back on. The rustling I can hear behind me indicating that he is doing the same.

The awkwardness makes me cringe. I have no idea what to do now. I just face-fucked Danny Covington and now he's doing a walk of shame out of my apartment.

When he is ready, we walk towards the front door.

I don't look up as I open it. A strong hand appears over my head and closes the door before his hard body backs me up to it. "Stop freaking out, freckles," he says gently, catching my eye.

"I'm not freaking out," I mumble.

He smirks knowingly. "When can I see you again?" he asks, running his nose along my neck. It's unfair of him to expect me to remember things like a calendar whilst his sinful fingers trace my stomach.

"You'll see me tomorrow." I gulp as he presses a wet kiss to my neck, the hickey he left me with finally fading.

"When can I see you like this?"

"Uhm." Coherent thought goes out the door as his teeth descend onto my flesh, gently biting the same spot as if he wants his mark to remain etched on my skin.

"After work tomorrow, I'll be back here." Danny says, pulling away and looking into my eyes.

"Okay," I whisper breathless.

"Good," he says, pressing a gentle kiss to my lips.

Before I can formulate any other words, he pulls the door open and calls, "See you tomorrow, freckles," over his shoulder as he descends the apartment stairs.

I close the door behind me and take a deep breath. What have I gotten myself into?

Chapter 24

When the door to Anya's Parisian apartment slams behind me, my fingers itch for a cigarette and I pull my purple vape out of my pocket.

I had anticipated spending the whole day with Anya, or at least more than an hour or two. I wanted to fall asleep in a bed that smells like her, and drink coffee from a cup she uses everyday. I wanted to lounge on the couch and channel surf and wash my dishes in the sink in the kitchen. But instead, I ate her out on her couch and left.

It's so easy to be around her. I feel more myself with her than I've felt in a long time. Standing beside her and talking about what her life looks like back home —discussing future baby names, for gods sake — it's brought me back to earth with a thump. I could tell she was about to ask me why I was practically groping her Aunt's guitar and quickly changed the subject. But it's done nothing to alleviate the spark of energy that coursed through me when I plucked a string.

I wished I could swing it into my arms and play the songs that have filled the small blue notebook I bought that day we spent together. I haven't picked up a guitar since my father took mine away from me when I was seventeen. The *Better You Know* press tour was about to start and I asked my father if I could take it with me. He yanked it from my hand and said "You're an actor, not a singer, don't be so ridiculous." I never saw it again and still haven't bought a replacement. It's been ten years and I haven't picked up a guitar since.

The irony of me telling Anya to stop freaking out when I'm basically spiraling in a blueberry scented cloud of smoke on the street is not lost to me. A kernel of doubt has wedged itself behind my rib cage and I don't think I can ease it out.

I pause at the corner of her road. My feet feel heavy as I contemplate walking further away from her. My body is on the street but I left something behind in that cozy apartment. I rub my hand across my face, as if it will slap some sense into me. I should keep walking, leave before whatever faint line we have erected blurs even more than it already has.

I turn back the way I came.

A neighbor holds the building's door open so I easily slip through the foyer. I take long strides up the stairs until I'm suddenly standing at her door. I knock once, the door swings open, and Anya's surprised face peers up at me. Before she has a chance to speak, I take her freckled cheeks in my hands and press my lips to hers. Her shock gives way to desire as she sinks into me. My tongue explores her lips and her hands slide up my arms.

I pull away, her face cradled in my hands. I don't dwell on how right this feels. "I never got to see your bedroom." I press hungry kisses to her lips as I maneuver us backwards through the door.

"Hmm," she says, returning my kisses, "Silly me."

We walk in the direction of her room, our lips never more

than a whisper apart. She fiddles with the handle to her bedroom door and it swings open behind her. Her feet trip on the floor, but my arms cradle her closer to me. She's so slight against me I feel like we're floating towards the fluffy bed I spot over her shoulder.

I gently guide her towards it but she offers resistance, pushing me until I reach the wall. I thought I had taken the reins, but it appears I just handed her my leash.

My back presses to the wall, the cool brick offering no relief from the fire racing through my body. Anya explores me, pressing open mouthed kisses to my neck, her hands roaming my body until she fiddles with the button of my jeans.

She tugs at the material, dropping to her knees as my dick falls free.

She licks her lips and my head falls against the wall with a thud.

"It's only fair," she whispers against my skin, making my erection twitch. Whatever my mind could have conjured up to say is lost in a groan as her soft lips tease the head of my aching cock. She parts her lips before enveloping me in her warm mouth. Her nails scratch against my thighs as she works me, teasing and licking with every bob of her head. Her fingers creep closer, cupping my balls before joining her sinful mouth and working my shaft.

My hands fist themselves in her hair, the silky strands between my fingers. I take a shuddery breath as she speeds up her movements with a moan I can feel in the back of her throat.

"Good girl," I whisper as a shiver works its way up my spine.

Her legs spread with a whimper. The knowledge that this is affecting her as much as it is me sends me into a frenzy.

"Touch yourself."

Her hand falls from my thigh and slides into her underwear, the sight almost causing me to black out. My hands leave her hair and curve under her jaw. I tease my thumb along her bottom lip, pulling her away from my aching cock with an audible pop.

I plunge my thumb into her wet mouth and her eyelashes flutter. "Greedy girl." Her mouth tightens around my finger before I tug it free, sweep her into my arms and carry her to the bed. I kick off my jeans and she shimmies out of her clothes. Her naked body falls back on the bed, her hair fanning across the white sheets.

"Beautiful," I say reverently as my hands cup her breasts, my fingers flicking her pebbled nipple.

I fish a condom out of my wallet. Anya sits up and takes it from my hand, ripping the package with her teeth and rolling it onto me. I chase her back to the bed and notch myself at her entrance. As her heat envelops me, I bury my face in her neck, kissing her soft skin.

Her hand finds its way into my hair and when she pulls, it's enough to make me come right then, but I hold off, desperate to feel her shatter around me. I piston my hips into hers as my fingers reach for her bundle of nerves, moving in a way I know will drive her wild.

She whimpers into my mouth as I clasp her lips with mine, my fingers in time with my thrusts until her head falls back and her mouth drops open. Her walls flutter around me as I ride her through her orgasm, watching the flush behind her freckles deepen with pleasure.

Without waiting for her to return to earth, my hand finds her soft thigh and positions her leg against her chest. The new angle allows me deeper, sinking further into her delicious heat, and it's not long before my orgasm wrecks my body.

I collapse on top of her, careful not to crush her with my weight as we catch our breath.

She pecks a kiss to my forehead and I think I've died and gone to heaven. I never want to move. I want to stay cradled in her arms forever.

Eventually, I roll off her. Pressing a soft kiss to her lips I quickly dispose of the condom before returning to her, spread across her bed just as I left her.

I open my arm and she burrows into my side.

"I'm glad you came back," she says, breathlessly.

"I bet you are," I quip.

She taps my chest lightly before peering up at me. I could spend the rest of my life kissing this girl and it would scarcely be a hardship. God, I'm so fucked.

"Are you hungry?" she asks.

"Sure."

Her naked body clambers over me. She pulls her clothes back on and holds out a hand to me.

I let her tug me out of bed. I pull my boxers on but don't allow myself to touch the other clothes strewn around the room. If I let myself get dressed, I'm one step closer to leaving again.

I follow her to the kitchen. She rises to her tiptoes to peer into the top cupboard, pulling out a baguette.

"I'm surprised you don't have a chef."

Her head tilts back with a groan. "Oh my *god*, get another joke."

I laugh and press a kiss to her forehead, content to watch her make me a sandwich.

Later, as the sun starts to set from through the Juliet balcony, we lie tangled together watching TV. Claudette's guitar rests on the stand to the left. I blame the French show that I can't understand for the way my eyes can't stray from it. I feel ridiculous, I'm like a kid in a candy store. I could walk out of this apartment and buy myself a hundred Gibson's right now, but that beat up acoustic won't leave me alone.

"Do you play?" I turn to Anya, surprised until I realize the voice was mine.

She blinks at me confused. "Huh?"

I clear my throat. "Never mind." My spine locks up with embarrassment and I want to sink into the floor.

"Play what?" Anya glances around the room before her eyes land on the instrument that is actually just starting to piss me off. "Guitar? No, don't have the patience. I don't even think Claudette plays, I think it's more for decoration."

I nod and turn my attention back to the TV, hoping she'll move on.

She doesn't. "Do you?"

I shift uncomfortably. "Uh, no."

"Liar."

I pull at my top. "Not really."

"Why are you being so weird?"

"I'm not being weird."

"Yes, you are." She swings her legs off my lap and pads across the room. Swinging the guitar into her hands like it's no big deal, like it's not a momentous obstacle to overcome. She hands it to me. "Play me something."

"I can't."

"Fine, I'll play it."

She settles in next to me and my chest eases.

Anya fiddles with it in her lap, situating it across her thighs. She clears her throat dramatically before playing a very out of tune rendition of the opening chords of Deep Purple's Smoke On The Water. Her triumphant grin when she finishes causes laughter to bubble in my chest.

"And that's all I got," she laughs, before handing it to me again. "Come on, your turn."

Suddenly, the weight of the instrument is in my hands. It's not as heavy as it should be. It settles in my arms like an old friend. I fiddle with the tuning pegs for too long. Anya settles into the arm of the couch, giving me her full attention.

I don't speak, scared the words that fall out of my mouth will be another refusal.

Nerves flutter in my stomach but my fingers tease the strings, until I'm playing a timid rendition of Paolo Nutini's *Better Man*. It was one of the first songs I taught myself, watching tutorials online and practicing until calluses appeared on my fingers. It feels right that that was the first song I played for myself and it's the first one I'm playing for her. The lyrics tumble through my head, but I don't dare voice them.

It's only when I reach the final verse that I quietly start to sing the words. My voice is raspy, unused after so long, but as the lyrics fall out of my mouth, I feel something in my chest wake up.

The song ends and I finally dare a glance at Anya. She beams at me. "How long have you had that in your back pocket?"

I huff a laugh. "Uh."

"Play me another one."

"I haven't played in a while."

"How long is a while?"

"About ten years."

She tilts her head. "Why?"

I shift awkwardly, but tighten my grip on the guitar. "My father didn't like it."

I almost expect to see sympathy dance across her face, instead it's anger that scrunches her eyebrows together. "Y'know, the more I learn about your dad the more I think he's a giant dick."

I laugh. Anya rises to her knees and crawls towards me, pressing a gentle kiss to my lips.

"Play me another."

So I do.

Chapter 25

ANYA

It's easy to forget my concerns about the quasi-situationship we've stumbled into. The shoot days are long. By the end of the day, it's easy for Danny to follow me into my apartment and collapse into bed.

We've stayed at the hotel a few times, mostly if the location is closer, anything to be alone as soon as possible. It's like the minute the door closes, shrouding us in privacy, we can finally be ourselves.

Today, after waking up with his arms wrapped around me and legs tangled together, we're spread out in the living room. I'm pretending to read a book whilst Danny fiddles with Claudette's battered acoustic guitar. The minute I forced it into his arms, I watched him come alive. He's spent all our time off-set with either me or that guitar in his arms. I would be jealous if I wasn't so turned on. I've never been into musicians and I've never been into famous rich boys. But I'm apparently *very* into Danny Covington.

I read the same sentence ten times, my mind falling instead on Danny's fingers teasing the guitar, the music he's playing preventing me from thinking of anything else.

He starts playing the refrain of a familiar song but I can't quite remember the name.

"Wait, what is this?" I ask.

He grins and keeps playing, not giving me an answer.

He keeps playing, and hums along with the melody.

Suddenly it clicks. I gasp, "Ah that's so *cheesy*," I wail as I finally recognize the song *Our Last Summer*.

Danny cackles and I throw the cushion from behind my head at him. He catches it with a laugh and my hands itch to grab a camera and immortalize the moment.

He grabs the cushion and rests his guitar on the floor. He crosses over to the couch I'm draped across and lightly drops the cushion on my face.

I lift my head so he's able to sit beneath me and I lay my head in his lap.

"When will you play outside?" I ask, looking up at him.

"I had the window open," he says as he starts to play with my hair.

"You know what I mean," I say looking up at him.

He's silent for a moment. "I like this, playing for you, making you smile. It's enough." He gently tugs at my bottom lip trying to distract me.

He should share his gift with the world and he knows it. "For now," I say, dropping it, pressing a kiss to the thumb resting against my lips.

"For now," he promises as he leans down and replaces his hand with his mouth. I reach up and grab the back of his head to keep him with me, and all thoughts of anything else disappear.

"Play me another." I tug on his earlobe.

"I should have never told you I can play. I feel like a jukebox,"

Danny says dramatically.

I laugh and sit up on my knees on the couch. "Come on, just one more song."

"I have a better idea." He leans towards me for a kiss, trailing his hand along my thigh. I lean my head back as he presses a kiss to my neck and his hand creeps higher. Ignoring the spark in my belly, I grab his hand. "Please."

Danny laughs, "Fine, freckles."

I smile as he fetches his guitar and settles back next to me. "Any requests?" he asks, as he starts to strum a mindless refrain that fills the room with magic.

There is no question what I want to hear, "One of yours." I rest my head on my hand.

His fingers still over the strings. "Pass, pick again."

"I want a Danny Covington original."

"Anya," Danny groans.

"Please."

He looks at me with a sigh, "Okay, but no laughing."

"As if."

I bite my lip as his brow furrows in concentration, his fingers gently picking across the strings. I have heard him sing before, but this is different. This is all him.

Danny doesn't look up at me once whilst he sings, concentrating on his guitar and the words sliding out of his mouth like butter. As he hits the last note, his voice trails off and he glances in my direction. He can't meet my eye.

He clears his throat and rises with his guitar.

I realize I haven't said anything. "Danny", I croak.

He runs a hand through his hair as he glances at a spot over my shoulder.

I grab his hand and tug until he collapses back on the couch.

"Danny," I repeat, "That was–that–"

"It's okay, you can say the truth," Danny says, picking imaginary lint off his jeans.

"Danny, that was beautiful." His head rises.

"You're just saying that."

"No, I'm not. That was incredible. You need to do this. This is what you're supposed to be doing. You sound like that and you *write* like that."

He looks like he wants to argue, but I swing my leg across his lap and straddle him. His hands grasp my hips and rocks me towards him. The hardness I can feel sends a jolt of lightening up my body. I grab his head and tilt his face back. "I mean it."

Danny rests his forehead against mine. "Thank you," he whispers, before catching my lips in his.

I can't help the moan that escapes as he wraps his arms around me. Our kiss heats up, our tongues furiously dancing as we cling to each other. I let him go, trailing kisses down his neck and smiling at the strangled noise that escapes him.

"Danny," I say, into the juncture of his neck.

"Hmm?"

"Play me another."

He tilts my face back to his. "Later," he murmurs around my lips as he lifts me seamlessly and walks to the bedroom.

Chapter 26

The shoot is starting to wind down. Danny has nearly finished his scenes, reduced to just a number of hours a day or occasionally no days at all. I'm not needed on set when Danny isn't there and days we're not, I notice a day less pay in my paycheck. It's hard to complain when I'm making more money than I've ever seen in my life, and spending my extra days off in a five-star hotel room with a man I'm pretty sure I'm falling too hard for.

It's becoming exceedingly rarer to stay at The Belle Palais mainly because Danny wants to be as far away as possible from Callum at all times. But today I am not in the mood to wait the extra half an hour after wrap for Danny to get over to my place. I follow him out of the car with much fanfare, loudly discussing 'logistics' as I trail him through the lobby.

As soon as his hotel room door closes behind us, I'm on him.

He laughs against my lips as his arms come up to my hips. "At least buy me dinner first."

"Shut up," I say, tugging at his shirt. We stumble back to the bed, hands roving.

"I'm not complaining," Danny says when I finally pull his

t-shirt over his head.

The sound of the door knocking causes us to disconnect like snapped elastic. I look at Danny through wide eyes.

"Jaques?" I hiss.

He shrugs helplessly as he tugs his shirt back over his head. I stand and quickly flatten my hair, readjusting my crinkled top.

I watch Danny as he peers through the peephole. He sighs before he glances at me. "It's my sister."

His *sister*? That is very much worse than Jaques. I spin in place, desperately looking for a way to look casual and not like I was seconds away from nudity. I end up near the en suite door. Maybe it will look like I've just popped in to use the bathroom. Which is potentially more embarrassing than the nudity.

"She'll be cool," Danny reassures me as he swings the door open and I hear a posh voice say, "Hello, hello."

Danny exchanges cheek kisses with the blonde at the door before gesturing to where I cower in the corner of the room, desperately praying I've suddenly developed the power of invisibility.

"This is Anya," he says.

Pip Covington looks at us with a raised brow, her face screaming *busted*. She pulls off her glamorous sunglasses and blue eyes the same shade as Danny's sparkle at me.

"Hi, Anya," Pip says, breaking out in a smile aimed at Danny. The kind of shit-stirring smile that is reserved purely for siblings.

"Anya, is my—"

"I'm Danny's assistant," I blurt out, ignoring his wince.

Pip's grin grows, nodding her head.

"Your t-shirt is on inside out." Pip taps Danny's shoulder as she squeezes past him and towards me.

Horror spears through me. Definitely busted.

"How are you finding Paris?" Pip asks me in a friendly voice. I find myself searching for a catty undertone, something that would make her bubbly personality fake.

"Oh uhm." I'm thrown off now. Aren't models supposed to be bitchy? "Yeah it's nice," I finish off lamely, glancing at Danny over her shoulder.

"How long are you here for?"

"Oh uh — until wrap." I run my hand through my hair. "Or well until Danny leaves, I guess." I swallow my tongue. "Not that I'm like *following him* or anything just that well — I'm, y'know his assistant so when he's not around, I don't really have a job. So I'll be here until Danny, uh, leaves." Kill me. Please.

I chance a look at Danny and see that he's biting his smile back and failing. I glare at him until he eventually steps forward and intervenes.

"What are you doing here, Pip?"

"Just a quick visit." She flaps her hand in his direction and takes a seat on the armchair. "What are you planning on doing after this?"

Danny's groan tells me that that question is directed my way. I stare at his sister blankly as she smiles at me.

"I don't know," I say, trying to not let it sound like a question. No matter how nice his sister is, it's pretty clear she's trying to figure me out. Trying to decide if I'm using her brother to get a leg up in my career. It's nothing I haven't already thought every person who finds out about us will think, but it still hurts.

"Phillipa," Danny says sternly, taking a seat on the small settee and pulling my frozen body down next to him. "Back off."

"I'm only asking!"

"It's okay," I say, my back straightening. I look Pip in the eye. "I don't know what I'm doing next. I'm still figuring out what I want to do. Where to go from here. This job isn't exactly…what I was expecting." I tuck my hair behind my ears. Danny's hand follows mine, running his fingers across my neck and gently brushing my hair over my shoulder. Claiming me.

I'm not sure if any of what I said makes any sense but Pip beams at me. "I like you." She turns to Danny. "I like her. I like this."

Uhm.

"Look, I know my brother. He's not one to fool around with the help, so you must mean something to him."

Danny ducks his head as I pull my eyes away from his whirlwind of a sister.

"How long has this been going on?"

I turn to Danny with wide eyes. I've already handled my interrogation, now it's his turn.

He rubs his hand across his face. "Jesus Pip, please chill out."

"I am chill!" Pip exclaims. "Am I not allowed to be happy for you? Honestly Anya, you should have seen him before. It was like living with a feral cat."

I can't help the conspiratorial grin that takes over my mouth as Danny groans.

"So?" Pip asks, glancing between the both of us.

I keep my mouth shut as Danny says. "It's new."

"This is so exciting." Pip says practically beaming with glee.

"Anyway, the reason I came is to invite you out with me and Cassie tonight. Anya, of course, you're more than welcome to come."

Danny and I share a glance.

He clears his throat. "We don't usually," –he runs his hands through his hair–"go out."

Tamping down on the disappointment rising in my belly, I say, "Honestly don't worry about me! You guys go and enjoy!" I hope they can hear my exclamation marks.

Danny's lip twitches and Pip buts in. "We'll just find somewhere private. Cassie is staying with her awful mother, in a room, not a suite. But maybe we could meet here?" She glances around the room.

Danny nods in agreement before my mouth blurts, "We can use my place."

Danny looks at me with a blinding smile.

"Perfect," Pip exclaims, clapping her hands. "Text me the address and I'll see you there." In a flurry Pip clasps my hands and presses kisses to my hot cheeks.

As soon as the door closes, Danny laughs at me. I throw a cushion at him and cover my face with my hands.

He catches it. "You are so cute."

I moan helplessly behind my palms. "Please tell me I haven't invited a supermodel over to my apartment tonight."

"You haven't invited a supermodel to your apartment." He tugs my hands away from my face and maneuvers me so I'm perched on his lap. "You invited a supermodel and her pop star best friend."

I look at him confused. "Huh?"

"Cassie." Danny says slowly as if I should know who–

"Shut the fuck up," I shout, shooting to my feet. "*Cassandra?*"

Cassandra — *Cassie* — is currently the biggest selling female artist, selling out stadium tours and crashing ticketing systems. And she's coming to *my* apartment.

"Oh my god. I'm going to throw up." Danny tugs me into his arms.

"They're both harmless," he says, pressing a kiss to my forehead.

"We weren't supposed to tell anyone," I mumble into his shirt, as his arms come around me and pull me tighter.

"Pip already knew something was up," he admits. I look up at him and rest my chin on his chest. He looks up, "She's been bugging me for a few weeks now. She says I sound happy or something like that." He won't look me in the eye but my mouth widens with glee.

"I make you sound happy?" I ask.

He tugs my hair, tilting my head back.

"Or something like that." He brushes his lips to mine and I sink into his arms. I pull him closer until we're moving, the back of my thighs hitting the mattress.

He cradles me as I fall backwards, his fingers tracing the sliver of skin between my shirt and jeans.

*⁂

Danny sufficiently distracted me from the impending disaster, but now as I race around my apartment picking up random bits of clutter and desperately cleaning the bathroom, I can't help but spiral.

"I've never seen you like this," Danny says, leaning against the door frame of the bathroom as I frantically clean the shower. "I highly doubt Cassie will need to shower, but I'm sure she will appreciate the effort."

I glare at him. "You are so not funny. You could always help."

"I helped an hour ago when you were deep cleaning the kitchen, and I've dusted and vacuumed everywhere. Which I'm pretty proud of because that French vacuum cleaner was a very difficult contraption." He steps towards me and takes my marigold clad hand. "I think you need to relax, freckles. They're normal people."

I sigh. "You're right." I drop my sponge. "You're right. I'm just stress cleaning."

Danny presses a kiss to my forehead and grabs his phone to check the time. "Pip texted saying they're on their way."

"*What?*" I blurt, "but I'm not ready."

"You look fine!" Danny says as I start to push him out of the bathroom.

I huff. "You are such a man."

He allows me to push him into the hall with a laugh. "I'm going to order the food," he says through the door.

I don't respond, instead ripping my clothes off and stepping into my nice clean shower.

I don't think I've ever got ready so fast in my whole life. Which is probably a good thing, as I have no time to panic about a supermodel, a pop star and my maybe-boyfriend eating dinner in my apartment.

Boyfriend? Where did that come from?

I have no time to dwell on the thought. I can hear Danny greet them at the door, welcoming them in as if he's done it thousands of times. By the time I emerge from my bedroom, dressed casually in jeans and a t-shirt, my palms are sweating as I approach the group.

Pip spots me first, swallowing a sip of wine. "There you are!" She hugs me as if we've known each other for years and not a number of hours. "This is Cassie." She gestures to Cassandra, who is already sitting on the couch and chomping on chips and dip. I wave awkwardly, unsure what to do with my hands.

Pip separates from me and I gravitate to Danny's side. He wordlessly hands me a glass of wine before I sit next to him. I take a large sip to cool my nerves.

"I was just telling the guys about Aunt Claudette."

"Yeah, we spotted the fertility statue," Cassie laughs.

I giggle. "Yeah, hopefully that's a dud." I freeze. Please say I didn't just reference having sex with my secret maybe-boyfriend.

I turn, wide eyed to Danny who, quite rudely, laughs at my expense. Taking pity on me, he presses a kiss to my palm and says, "We've ordered Chinese."

I take another gulp of wine.

"I'm dying for a duck roll." Cassie groans. "My mother hasn't let any food touch my hand unless it's made out of water or lettuce." She raises her glass and takes a sip.

Pip and Danny share a loaded look. "How long is your mother here for?"

Cassie leans back in her seat. "Same as me. The only reason I was able to get away from her tonight is because I said I was meeting up with you guys. She just doesn't know we're having a greasy takeaway instead of a five-star meal at Le Cinq."

I feel my cheeks pink. Maybe I should have let Danny go without me to a posh restaurant, instead of hiding away inside drinking store-bought wine.

Pip nudges Cassie. "You don't even like Le Cinq. You said the shellfish was gross."

Cassie waves her hand, the wine sloshing in her glass. "Which is why this is so much better."

Danny's palm finds my knee and squeezes. It's strange

letting him touch me so casually when we've been monitoring every glance as if someone will jump out and point at us accusingly. The warmth of his palm makes me curse the jeans I'm wearing for providing a barrier between his skin and mine. My gaze follows his arm up to his strong bicep to see his blue eyes staring at me with a wink. I get lost in them for moments before Cassie's voice snaps me out of my trance.

"How's it going with McBride?"

Everyone tenses. I know Danny has a history with Callum, which is pretty obvious from every interaction they've ever had and his vague warning to stay away from him, but I didn't think Cassie would bring it up.

Danny pulls his hand from my knee and reaches for the wine. "As you would expect." He takes a swig.

Pip runs her hand through her hair. "Just leave it alone, Danny."

Danny raises his hands innocently. "I wish I could but he's like a bad smell. Always hanging around."

It's fascinating to see Danny in this environment. I only really know what he's like on set with people he's only just started warming up to, and what he's like with me. I know who he really is underneath and it makes my heart swell to watch him banter with Pip and Cassie.

"I just think—" Cassie starts before she's interrupted by the buzzer.

"I'll get it." Pip jumps up quickly running from the room. "Wait," I hear. "Anya, what do I do?"

I follow her with a laugh and see her holding the dated intercom phone with confusion.

I take it from her, "*Bonsoir, quatre etage si'l vous plait.*" I place it back on the receiver.

"I wish I could speak French," Pip says wistfully.

"I can teach you if you like." I offer.

Pip grins. "It's a date!"

The food arrives and we tuck in, eating out of foil cartons, not bothering with dishware. I would have thought this group would only eat off fine china and fancy silverware, but it all feels so…normal.

"How's the album going?" Danny asks Cassie.

She groans. "It's going somewhere. I was so sure I wanted to do this one on my own and now that I am, I realize why I've always worked with a bunch of people."

"Have you finished any songs?" Pip asks, around a spring roll.

Cassie shrugs, "A few. There's one in particular that is really pissing me off. I've got the gist, but can't figure it out."

"Maybe we can help," Pip says. "We've had enough to drink that I'm sure we'll be helpful."

Cassie laughs and I pipe up. "I have a guitar. Danny plays it all the time."

Pip and Cassie look at Danny so fast I'm surprised they don't get whiplash. "He does?" Pip blinks owlishly.

Danny ducks his head. "Only a little."

I furrow my brow. "You're really good Danny." It's his sister, surely she's heard him play before.

"I didn't know you were playing again," Pip says.

There's a telltale blush on his cheeks. "It's a uh," – a glance at me – "recent thing."

It dawns on me. Although Danny and Pip are close now, there's a very big part of his life that he's kept to himself. Until now.

"Well, let's see," Cassie says. "Maybe you'll be able to pick up on what I'm missing."

I glance at Danny trying to apologize with my eyes. His crinkle softly at the corners and I know I'm forgiven. I grab Claudette's guitar and I hand it to Cassie.

She strums a tune and sings along, the lyrics sound disjointed even to my amateur ears. "And then I have this riff but no lyrics yet." The tempo changes and she hums along.

I try to remain cool, but when the biggest pop star in the world is workshopping her newest song in my living room, it's almost enough for me to pinch myself. I sit back resting my arm on the top of the couch and sipping my wine, hoping I'm portraying my nonexistent aloofness. I look at Danny. He's leaning forward, staring intently at the guitar on Cassie's lap as if he can see the sounds coming out of it.

He sits back and pinches his lip with his fingers. Sat on opposite sides of the couch, he catches my eye. I lean my head on my arm and smile at him as Pip and Cassie talk quietly over the gentle music she plays. I feel like I can read his mind. *Should I?* I smile at him. This is it.

He nods to himself and clears his throat. "May I?" Cassie stops playing and looks at him.

She hands the guitar over, and I watch as he settles it in his lap. "Sing what you have," he tells Cassie.

She looks at me and I shrug.

Danny starts playing. I would have thought he'd seen the sheet music, but knowing this is Cassie's demo, it's impossible. He parrots the chords Cassie played earlier. Her surprise leads her to stumble on the first line, but she picks it up quickly. When it gets to the empty refrain, Danny opens his mouth.

Shivers break over my spine as I watch him make magic. Pip's jaw is on the floor but Cassie's eyes are lit up, and she follows where he's leading her, their voices mingling. Eventually he stops and looks at me. I don't even bother hiding my grin.

"Holy shit," Cassie says. "How did you do that?"

Danny shrugs. "I just picked it up." He glances at Pip, who's still shocked.

"Wow," she says.

I reach out and run my fingers across his temple. "That was amazing."

Cassie pulls out her phone and presses record. "Let's do it again."

Chapter 27

DANNY

I've never sang for anyone other than Anya, so playing for my sister and Cassie feels surreal.

As Cassie stumbled through her song, I felt my heart beat pounding in my chest. Something inside me was telling me *this is it, go for it.* But then a voice that sounded like my father did it's best to stamp it down. It was only after Anya caught my eye, and I saw in her expression encouragement–*love*–I knew I could do it.

Every time Cassie or I would create a lyric that was just right, I felt like I was on top of the world.

That evening, sitting in a room with some of the people I love the most in the world, finally doing something I've wanted to do for the longest time, I felt like my heart would burst out of my chest.

Anya slots seamlessly in with Pip and Cassie. She and Pip spent the evening alternating between listening to us and giggling to each other over the rest of the wine.

Still, when Cassie asks me to perform on the song as a duet, I stumble. Could I really make that last jump?

"Think about it," Cassie says, pressing a kiss to my cheek as we say our goodbyes. "I'm going to take this to the studio, but even if you don't want the duet, you'll need to come in when you're back in LA."

I nod, unable to find the words.

Pip hugs me tightly, whispering in my ear, "I'm happy for you, Dan," before pulling Anya into a bear hug. "Next time I see you we're going for brunch. *Au revoir!*"

Anya laughs and promises to stay in touch. As soon as the door closes behind them, I have my girl in my arms and her soft lips under mine.

She looks up at me with a twinkle in her eye and I almost say those three little words at the tip of my tongue. I swallow them down before they escape and get me in trouble.

"I need to clean up," Anya says resting her head on my chest. "If I don't do that before we start this"–she waves a hand between us– "I will never do it."

I laugh and press a kiss to her hair. "I'll help."

Anya gathers the empty wine bottles and I pick up the guitar I left leaning against the side table.

"You were amazing," she says, cradling the bottles in her hand.

"Thank you." For everything.

She smiles and bustles around the room collecting our mess. I put the guitar back in its place and gather the wine glasses. Loading dishes into the dishwasher shouldn't be a new experience, but helping Anya clean up after my family visited feels domestic. It feels like this is what we could have everyday. We could close up the house before brushing our teeth side by side at the sink and climbing into bed together, knowing that tomorrow we get to do it all over again. I don't know why it feels like such a far-fetched dream, but the more time I spend with Anya, the more real it feels.

Once the room is set to rights and we turn off the lights, I can't take it any longer. I cradle Anya's face in my hands. She looks up at me with those big hazel eyes and I almost say the words floating at the tip of my tongue.

Instead, I take her to bed and show her.

Chapter 28

DANNY

When my sister falls in love, she falls in love hard. Which is why a few days after she met Anya for the first time, she sends me a detailed itinerary signed *'Have fun xoxo'*.

Scanning the itinerary in the back of the car with Anya, I laugh under my breath. Pip definitely goes all out.

"What?" Anya asks from beside me. She still insists on sitting far away from me and never touching. Oblivious to the looks Jaques sends me after every excuse she gives to follow me upstairs.

I wink at Anya and lean forward, "Jaques, can we go straight to Anya's?"

She splutters beside me and her hand grabs my shirt pulling me back to my seat.

"No problem," Jaques says, seamlessly turning up a side street to head to the sixteenth.

"What are you doing?" Anya hisses.

"It's a surprise."

She gapes at me and it doesn't take long until we're pulling up outside her apartment. She jumps out the car, closing the door firmly behind her. I hang back to speak quietly to Jaques before keying in her code and following her up the stairs. She's left the apartment door ajar for me and I can already hear her banging about inside.

"I can't believe you," she yells from the kitchen, rummaging through her cupboards. "What is Jaques going to think?"

I can't help the chuckle that escapes as I lean against the door frame, "He's going to think 'it's a good thing I know the way because I've been dropping Danny off there for weeks.'"

Anya spins, the cupboard door slamming shut.

I step closer to her and close her gaping mouth with my finger, "How did you think I was getting here every night?"

She blows out a breath. "Bike?"

I laugh, "I wouldn't be caught dead on one of those things."

She groans and rests her head against my chest. "That's three people that know about us now. We were supposed to keep it between us."

I press a kiss to the top of her head, her shampoo invading my nostrils. After spending time with my sister and Cassie, seeing how well Anya could fit in with my life outside of these four walls, I don't know if I want to keep it between us any more.

I just need to wait for Anya to catch up. I've waited my whole life for her, what's a few more weeks?

"Jaques hasn't spilled the secret yet." I tilt her head back, cradling her head in my hands and pressing a soft kiss to her lips. "Do you trust me?"

"Yes."

"Good, get ready to go."

"Go where? Back to your hotel?"

"I thought you said you trusted me?"

"I do trust you but first we're telling people—"

"Three people, freckles."

"—and now you want me to go outside—"

"Anya," I cut her off, "We're not going to walk naked down the Champs-Élysées. It'll be fine."

An hour later, Jaques pulls up outside a glamorous storefront. I step out first, and offer a hand to Anya who squints at me suspiciously. She looks up and down the empty street furtively before taking my hand and climbing out of the car. The sun has almost disappeared behind the tall buildings and the street is quiet.

"*Bonsoir, je suis Gérard.*" The gray haired clerk holds the door open for us. As soon as we step inside the elegant store, he clicks the lock behind us. Anya's head spins at the sound and turns to me with wide eyes.

"Danny," she hisses, inching closer. "What the hell is going on?"

I pull her closer by the hand, and whisper in her ear. "There's no one in here apart from Gérard. It's all Pip's idea."

"*What's* Pip's idea?" she presses urgently.

I gesture to the room, "Whatever you want."

Her brows scrunch adorably. "I am so confused."

I laugh and pull out my phone, quickly texting Pip for backup.

Instantly, Anya's phone vibrates. She reads it quickly before showing me the screen.

Pip: Go crazy! On me xx

Pip: Enjoy!!

"How did she even get my number?" Anya grouses, as her fingers fly across the screen.

"Come on." I say, tugging her further into the store. Luxury handbags are displayed on mahogany shelves and clothes are evenly spaced on delicate rails. I recognize some of the items from Pip's never ending closet, and I can't imagine Anya will want any of it. "What would you like?"

"What do you *mean* what would I like? I'd like to not be here." She glances at Gérard. "No offense."

I laugh and gesture more at the racks. "Pip is a brand ambassador, anything you want is complimentary."

Her eyes bug out of her head, "Anything? In the whole store?"

"Yes, freckles. You could take one of the mannequins if you want but you'll have to explain to Jaques."

"This feels so…wrong."

"What will feel wrong is the harassment Pip will put us through if we walk out of here with nothing."

"Well, what are you going to get?"

"Nothing."

Anya throws her hands up. "This is ridiculous."

I laugh, "What about these?" I direct her attention to the row of handbags lining a delicate trestle table.

She follows suspiciously and I gesture to the table.

Anya sighs and rests her fingers across the soft leather. "I'm more of a tote bag girl, I have way too much stuff to carry." She flips the lid of a clear acrylic purse. "I don't understand this one, everyone would be able to see your tampons."

I told Pip that I didn't think Anya was a luxury fashion lover, but she wouldn't be told. If it wasn't for the thought of finally being alone with Anya outside of her apartment or my hotel, I would have told Pip to back off. Plus, it's amusing watching Anya be forced into accepting some generosity.

"Do you like it?" I ask in her ear.

She turns to me with a glare. "What do you think?"

"I think if you don't get something, Gérard here is going to report back to Pip that her personal guest hates their lines. She'll be devastated."

Her eyes narrow as she hisses, "So you're going to force me to buy a ridiculously expensive see-through bag, just so your sister doesn't get upset?"

I shrug, "You said it."

She huffs dramatically, "I know where she gets it from."

She puts the bag down and wanders the store. She keeps her hands tucked by her sides as she wanders across the dark green carpet, barely touching anything like she's in a museum. I watch as she sidesteps Gérard awkwardly and heads to the fragrance section. I step behind her and watch as she sniffs each bottle of perfume reluctantly. The third one she lifts to her nose twice before spraying it on a delicate wrist.

I clasp her hand and investigate for myself. My hand could wrap around both of her wrists easily. I bring her wrist to my nose and inhale, the floral notes invading my senses but not quite masking the sweet scent that is still distinguishably Anya.

I glance up to see her attention is fixed on where we're joined. I press a quick kiss to the inside of her wrist, my tongue licking at the cloying scent.

"Hmm," I say quietly, "I like it." I run my nose against her arm, pressing gentle kisses along her skin, smiling when goosebumps erupt in my wake.

She gulps and I release her, stepping to the side to gesture to Gérard who quickly escapes to the store room to grab a bottle of the perfume.

"Are we done?" Anya says, her pink tongue flicking against her lip.

"You have to get something from Pip."

"I just did!"

"No," I say, resting my hand on her hip and whispering in her ear. "That was for me."

A tiny moan escapes as I press a kiss to her cheek. "Keep looking."

Chapter 29

Danny hovers behind me like a shadow, desperate for me to spend his money. If I wasn't so morally against wasting money on clothes that would only look good on a runway model, I would be having the time of my life. Or maybe if we were in a Le Creuset store so I could stack up on tiny espresso mugs.

I have my bottle of expensive perfume that I'll now forever associate with him, I'm more than ready to cut this little shopping trip short and escape home but he practically bars the exit.

I guess it's a nice thing that his sister has planned this for me. Like she's accepted me as Danny's…something. But maybe we should have a sit down and discuss what is and what isn't an adequate gift for a girl sleeping with your brother.

I eventually find a small collection of sunglasses. Jackpot. Surely these will be cheaper than the embroidered jackets with a price tag in the thousands. Danny hums appreciatively as I place each pair on my nose and present my face for his inspection.

"I like the second ones," he nods and I try them on again. They're not too big that they swallow my face and they're so dark it makes the already dim store almost pitch black.

"They're really light, I can barely feel them." I muse.

"Good." He pinches them gently off my nose and gestures to Gérard who quickly swipes them out of his hand.

"Are we done now?" A bottle of perfume and the cheapest item in the store, surely I've done my time.

He winks and hooks his arm around my waist guiding me out of the store. "Good job, freckles. Pip will be pleased."

Gérard hands my tiny shopping bags to Jaques and he turns to me, "Did you have fun?" he asks in English.

I grimace playfully, "I picked the cheapest thing in the store."

Jaques raises his eyebrows and glances at Danny. I turn to the man trying to usher me into the car. "Didn't I? The sunglasses weren't too expensive were they?"

I can see the smirk Danny is not attempting to hide.

"Were they?"

"Get in the car, freckles."

Chapter 30

DANNY

It's almost wrong to be on set. To be pretending to be someone else when I finally, *finally*, feel like myself. I've played music and people have encouraged me, I have the perfect girl warming my bed basically every night, and I'm firmly ignoring my fathers calls. It feels wrong to be doing anything else.

When I read the script sat at that conference table, I never imagined that my life could look so different. The resentment that weighed me down has lightened considerably thanks to the new direction Anya's steered me in. So even though I'd rather be anywhere else, I know that I can at least do a good job on this film. Not for myself and the career I can finally admit isn't what I want, but so I can make Anya proud.

The thing about a good mood is it can always turn bad. Mostly by the presence of the worst human in the world. McBride loves finding anything to get under my skin, to wind me up. And today, he's definitely found it.

I hand my phone to Anya before the scene starts. We don't even do anything suspicious, I just rest my fingers on hers and she sends me that dazzling smile. That happens all the time.

I turn to step to my mark and spot McBride's twisted grin.

Grimacing, I ignore him. The worst part of this job, by far, is having to pretend that I don't want to punch him in the face every time I share a screen with him.

I ignore him as the camera settles. Rachel calls action and we fall into the scene. It's only during the first break that Callum makes his approach.

"Heard your sister is in town."

I clench my jaw and stare at him, meeting his beady eyes. "Flying visit. She's long gone."

"That's a shame," he says. "Would have been great to say hello."

My hands clench at my sides. Pip doesn't need me working myself up over this prick. I glance over at Anya, who is staring straight at us as if she can diffuse the tension from across the room. I take a calming breath and turn my attention away from Callum, looking to Rachel for my cue.

Callum leans forward, covering his breast pocket where I know his mic is sitting, preventing anyone on the other end from hearing what he's about to say. "That girl of yours, Annie. Think she's up for a ride too?"

My eyebrows raise as fury laces through my body. "What did you say?" I don't bother to hide my mic.

He shoots me a wicked grin and gestures with his chin to the corner where I know Anya is resting. "I'm sure she'd be open to it, unless you don't like to share. I bet she'd look good pinned against a wall an—"

I see red. I can hear voices calling out to me around me, but I ignore them as my fist flies into his smug face. He staggers back from the hit. If I wasn't blind with rage, I'd probably notice the slimy grin he sends me before he pushes me back.

I grab his collar and pull him towards me. "Say that again,

prick."

Callum smiles. "I knew you were fucking her."

My arm pulls back ready to swing before it's grabbed. I don't know who pulls me off him but I don't care. I keep swinging.

"Enough," Rachel yells. I stop struggling enough to realize that I've socked one of the crew guys in the jaw. I try to apologize, but my tongue is heavy in my mouth. Over his shoulder, I see Anya, her eyes wide and shocked. I shake off the guy holding me up.

People flutter around McBride like flies on shit, shooting me wary glances and whispering. My cheek is swollen from where McBride got a hit in, but I'd be surprised if he's not got a loose tooth. My hands are buzzing with adrenaline.

Rachel raises her voice. "Okay, everyone back up."

I don't wait for anyone as I turn and storm off set. I can barely look at Anya as I rush past her. The fresh air rushes into my lungs and I take a shuddering breath. Base is empty as I stumble to my trailer. The lights are off but I collapse on the couch, trying to control my breathing.

Eventually, I vaguely hear the door open and feel soft hands running through my hair.

"Breathe, baby." Anya. Just her voice settles my pounding heart.

I clutch her fingers in mine. "How bad is it?"

She pauses. "You've been asked to stay in your trailer for now."

I nod slowly.

"What did he say to you?"

I look up at her. "You don't know?"

She shakes her head. "Sound guy didn't have his headphones in."

Thank god.
"Was it,"–she swallows– "was it about me?"
I tug her to me, burying my head in her stomach.
She kisses my forehead. "It's okay."

Chapter 31

I don't know what the fight was about, but I have a sinking feeling it was about me, if the sinister smile Callum shot me before he was swarmed by well-meaning first aiders tells me anything. I know that the opinion on set is that Danny's a loose cannon and this episode has just proven every rumor true.

I had watched Danny leave the set and stamped down on the urge to run after him. I needed to put out some fires so I headed into the thick of it.

"What the hell, Anya?" Rachel had whirled on me as soon as I reached her.

Michael and Gwendoline crowded around me. I felt like I had been pulled into the headteachers office to snitch on my friend.

"That was unacceptable," Michael spat, his venom making me flinch. "I knew he was a mistake."

I swallowed my tongue, my heart pounded in my chest but I refused to leave Danny undefended.

I raised my hands helplessly. "Putting them together was a bad idea, it was only a matter of time."

Michael ignored me, "I'm calling his agent."

"Get to his trailer and keep him there until we know what's happening." Rachel said.

Now, I sit on my knees next to Danny as his leg shakes. His phone buzzes in my pocket. I hand it to him and he takes a breath before answering and putting it on speaker. An American voice booms.

"Danny, it's Travis. Listen, I've just had Michael on the phone. I hear there's been a disagreement with McBride. I want you to not worry about it, you've only got five scenes left to shoot, two of those with McBride, so there's no way they'll get rid of you now. Even without your father's influence."

Danny winces and gets to his feet.

"Have you spoken to him?"

"Charles? Listen, don't worry about him. All you need to know is they're looking at rewriting your last two scenes with McBride, including today. You're wrapped for now and will have to take a mandatory pay cut for loss of filming time but apart from that, it's all fine. I'll let you know if I hear anything else."

Travis cuts the call without letting another word in. Danny rubs his face and takes a shaky breath.

"This is good, yeah?" I ask quietly.

He says nothing.

"Look," I approach slowly, like he's a stray cat I want to follow me home. "Forget what Callum said, forget Travis and your dad and all of them. Do you want to see this through? You can leave right now. End it here."

He finally lifts his head, those blue eyes shining. His eyes rove my face like he's memorizing it.

"I want to stay."

Chapter 32

DANNY

The ride back to the hotel is silent. Anya hustles me into the waiting car with little fuss. Thankfully, most of the crew have yet to return from set, so there's no one to gawk at the crazy guy who started a brawl in the middle of a scene. I lean my head against the back of the headrest and close my eyes.

I keep my head down when we leave the car and don't look up again until Anya unlocks the hotel door and gently tugs me inside.

"Come on, Rocky." I huff a laugh as Anya guides me to lie back on the bed. She burrows into my side and rests her head on my chest. She takes my right hand in hers and gently traces the angry red marks on my knuckles.

"At least you didn't break skin."

"Hmm."

Anya raises onto her elbow and peers down at me. "Okay, time to spill. What am I missing?"

I sigh. "It's a long story."

She rolls her eyes. "Well luckily, we've suddenly got the day off."

"I told you before that Pip and I haven't always been that

close." She nods. "We'd only see each other a few times a year, but we'd always stick to it. It was an obligation I guess. Even though we were practically acquaintances, we still felt like we should make an effort. We went for lunch one day and she looked so miserable. I couldn't get it out of her for ages, but eventually she told me. She'd met this guy at an event or something and had hit it off. McBride. I didn't know much about him, only that he had done that one TV show, but we weren't exactly in the same circles.

So obviously for her job, she does a lot of raunchy stuff and I guess he saw the proofs that morning and had started going off at her. Calling her a slut and a whore, shit like that."

"What the fuck?" Anya splutters, furious. "It's literally her job."

"That was my reaction too. I told her that he sounded like a fucking loser and that she should dump him. But I guess after that she went straight back to him. I didn't even know until it was suddenly all over the internet and they were getting photographed together. I had a bad feeling, so I started reaching out more, making more of an effort to be there for her. I started hanging out with her and Cassie, who also was really suspicious of him. She didn't tell us anything else that he might have done, but I knew a guy like that wouldn't just let that go.

At the end of last year, Cassie threw this huge New Years Eve party. Everyone was there and I finally meet McBride. I hated him already but he was so smug that night. He wouldn't leave Pip alone. It's like he wanted everyone there to know that they were together. Later that night, I had lost sight of her–both of them–and got this bad feeling. I went looking for them and eventually found them in a guest room. He had her pinned up against the wall by her upper arms. It could have been consensual but his knuckles were *white* with how tightly he was holding her. And you should have seen the look in her eyes. God, I've never seen her like that. She looked so *scared*.

I just lost it. Pulled him off her and started wailing on him. He started hitting me back and shoving me down the hallway until we ended up in the main room. I realized later that he led me back into the party so everyone could see me going batshit crazy. Pip was screaming, everyone was shouting and eventually we got pulled apart."

I sigh, my bloody knuckles playing with the strands of Anya's hair. "The next day, it's all over the internet that he caught me doing drugs and tried to help me, so I beat him up for his effort. Which really put his name on the map."

"I don't understand," Anya says, running her fingers through my hair. "Why didn't you or Pip say anything?"

I shrug. "I would rather I get slaughtered in the press than watch it happen to my sister. Who knows what they'd say about her."

Anya kisses me softly. "You're a good brother."

I scoff. "If I were a good brother, I would have never let her be with him in the first place."

"You did all you could, you were there for her when she needed it."

It's such a relief to get the whole truth off my chest. For a while, it was almost like I'd imagined the whole thing. When the whole world tells you who you are, it's easy for doubt to fester. "Well, we're close now, that's what matters."

"What did your parents say?"

I clench my jaw. "My mother didn't believe it. She's always preferred to keep her head buried, especially when it comes to

Pip. As long as she's pretty enough to be photographed, she's fine. My father…" I laugh with no traces of humor. "I have my suspicions he's started this whole production just to get me back in the same room as McBride."

"Why would he do that?" Anya asks quietly, disbelieving.

"That's dear old dad for you. Who knows why he does anything."

Anya shifts until she's closer, her body pressing against mine with a comforting weight.

"So what happened today?"

I groan. "He's been provoking me this whole time, trying to get me to snap again and give him exactly what he wants. And he finally got it."

"What did he say?"

Not happening. "I don't want to tell you."

"But it was about me?"

I nod slightly, watching as she bites her lip.

"God, it's not fair!" She rolls off the bed and starts pacing. "How is a guy like *that* able to be *that* much of a prick and everyone thinks *you're* the bad guy?"

I sit up and take her hand in mine. "As long as you don't think I'm a bad guy, that's all that matters." I tug her closer until she's straddling my thighs. I cradle her waist, pulling her closer until we line up perfectly. She melts into me, allowing me to take her weight. Her head rests on the crook of my shoulder and we lay quietly. I would hold her forever if I could.

Chapter 33

Danny wraps on set with an awkward tension. The film has another week or two before the official wrap, but as far as Danny and I are concerned, our time on *Accordance* is over. I'm a little sad that my first film job is over, but I'm mostly relieved. It's not a hardship to walk off the set of a film that Charles Covington is behind.

The day Danny finally told me what happened with Callum, it was like all the puzzle pieces slotted together. It's pretty clear to me that Callum is a pathetic fame chaser, but I can't ever forgive Charles for orchestrating this whole ordeal just to get some publicity. Of course, an anonymous source has already leaked that a fight broke out on set, halting production. Danny was quiet the day that came out and not even me waving the guitar in his face was enough to snap him out of it.

Danny hasn't left his trailer much since his return. I can't blame him and haven't done much to encourage him out. I collect our final catered lunch and bump into Jess at the craft table.

"Hey Anya." Jess greets me with a smile, piling bread onto her polystyrene plate. "It's so sad you won't be around anymore."

"Well you know, I go where Danny goes."

Jess laughs. "Hey you should come out tonight, a bunch of us are going to this bar in the tenth."

"Oh," I say. "Sure, that sounds fun."

"Nice, we'll be there from nine. I'll text you the details."

"I'll see you there."

After Danny's final scene, there is a polite smattering of applause. Gwen makes a small speech praising his performance, which he ducks his head for. Danny hands out a few gifts to the crew. And that's it. Danny is officially wrapped.

We bundle into Jaques' car once he's freed from set. When we pull up outside Danny's hotel, he stops at Jaques' window and hands him a wrapped box that I know contains a very expensive watch that he spent hours choosing. Jaques beams and we say our goodbyes.

In Danny's room, he collapses onto the bed, exhausted. I climb up next to him and rest my head on his chest. It's almost second nature now to go to him. To lay beside him as if I'm supposed to be there.

"So," I start. "All done."

We haven't discussed what happens to us after the film wraps. What happens to *this*. Production hasn't booked a return ticket for me yet, but I'm sure I'll get one soon.

"Yeah." His hand plays with my hair, twirling it through his fingers.

I can't bear the thought that this is it, that this is the last time I'll have him like this.

He clears his throat but before he speaks, I blurt out. "Let's go out tonight."

His brow crinkles, "Out?"

I sit up, "Yeah, Jess mentioned the crew are going for drinks and she invited me. We could go out with them, it won't be suspicious if everyone we've worked with for the past two months will be there."

"Oh." His eyes catch on my lips as I lick them. "Am I invited?"

"I'm inviting you. It will be a little weird, probably." Definitely. "But once people start drinking they'll get over it."

"You want to?"

"Yeah."

He brushes my hair behind my ear with a sigh.

"Let's do it."

***

The bar the crew have arranged to meet at is down a small side alley alongside the Canal Saint-Martin. The minute we walk through the crowded bar and find the corner commandeered by the crew, I know this is a bad idea. The group have pushed tables together in a haphazard horseshoe shape, surrounded by mismatched chairs and half empty glasses.

"Hey guys," I say to the group. Comically, everyone does a double take at the figure awkwardly hovering behind me like a socially inept shadow. "Can we join?"

Jess, bless her, jumps up, eager to ease the awkward, pregnant tension. "Of course, grab those chairs over there." Danny looks around and grabs the two chairs, dragging them into position.

We sit, glancing around the room. The atmosphere is tense, the crew unused to socializing with the grumpy, celebrity talent. I silently beg for a return to normal conversation.

"Olivia was just telling us about the hotel for the party scene." I'm going to nominate Jess for the OBE. Olivia launches into a rant about the grumpy hotel owner who kept adding charges and limiting rooms they could film in.

Out of the corner of my eye, I see Danny's jaw clench. Not one to be too upset by difficult location department situations, I can read his tension as embarrassment. But from the wary glances from the crew, I know his attitude is being mistaken for contempt.

I stand. "I'll get the next round in." A chorus of cheers respond.

Danny grabs my sleeve. "Don't leave," he hisses.

"I'll be two minutes. Just say something funny." The icy glare he gives me makes me smirk. I'm half tempted to sourly pat him on the head as I pass, and I can't resist running my fingers quickly through the fine hairs at the back of his neck. Cursing myself a fool and praying no one notices my lack of judgment, I wander towards the bar. It would be just my luck to accidentally expose our relationship to the whole crew right at the end of it. Maybe this is why we've never really ventured further than my apartment or his hotel room. The easy tactile relationship we nurtured in the dark is hard to hide in the light.

At the bar, I quickly remember the state of my bank account now I no longer have an income and curse myself for my generous plan. Still, I order two bottles of wine and a tray of tequila. As I rummage in my bag for my purse, I glance over my shoulder and see Danny slumped in his seat, playing on his phone.

My phone chimes.

Danny: Come back right now

I roll my eyes.

Another chime.

Danny: And bring wine.

Pocketing my phone, I tell the bartender in French, "Start a tab. My friend will pay."

He nods and passes me my drinks.

Triumphantly returning to the table, loud jeers sound as I place the tequila on the table.

"On a school night?" Devon asks.

"Not for me," I reply.

"We're in at one tomorrow Dev," someone says. "You'll make it."

I hand a shot to Danny.

"I think this is a bad idea," he mutters.

"Too late, you've got a tab." I cheerfully clink my shot glass to his and we throw the alcohol down our throats.

He holds eye contact and I feel heat lick down my spine with the tequila.

"Ah, of course, you're welcome."

I grin impishly and lick a drip of tequila from the corner of my lip. His eyes track the movement.

"Let's play a drinking game," Charlie, one of the camera guys, suggests. There are some mumbles of discontent, but I remember that Rosie's fool proof plan for diffusing awkwardness at a party is a good drinking game.

"Let's do it," I say.

Drinks are poured and seats are rearranged as Olivia announces we'll play Never Have I Ever.

"Never have I ever..." Olivia says, "broken a bone."

Glasses raise.

Someone else pipes up. "Never have I ever stolen anything from set."

One of the art department guys takes a guilty sip ignoring

the annoyed gasps of his team. "What! I wanted those cinnamon bon bons and we scrapped the scene anyway."

"Never have I ever…" The sound guy says, "been in a fight."

Everyone freezes and whips their head to Danny. He gives a self-deprecating laugh and makes a show of taking a drink. The sound guy laughs and claps him on the shoulder, the tension dissolving into friendly ribbing.

"Oh, I love this song!" Sadie says. "Let's dance."

Jess jumps up and grabs my hand tugging me onto the dance floor. I feel Danny's eyes on me as I sway to the music, the song so different to the romantic jazz from the club the night we got together. If I sway my hips a bit more than necessary, that's the tequila not me.

The night gets significantly more lax, with the lights turning dim and the music getting louder. People mingle between the seats and as more people arrive, the crew spreads out and creates a barrier against the general public. Maybe that is why Danny has eased up. He's even started a conversation with the camera guy next to him.

I sit close to Danny's side, having barely left his eyesight without him texting me and demanding I return. Despite trying to hold a conversation with one of the costume girls next to me, I keep an eye on the various crew. Every now and then, I spot the telltale signs of gossip, as people look at him and whisper to each other.

It's not uncommon for cast and crew to mingle after wrap, but it was a given that Danny Covington is too famous for it to not be talked about.

The man in question hasn't looked at me for a while, too engrossed in his conversation, but my whole body is burning in anticipation — or stress — that any second one of us will slip and all our colleagues will twig that I've been shagging the talent.

The leg I have pressed against Danny's starts to fidget as I sip my wine. Lightly, the side of his pinky finger grazes my bare leg and I freeze. Glancing at him out of the corner of my eye, he hasn't moved, just brushing his finger against my twitching knee, a silent command to still. My heart begins to pound, but I plant my feet firmly on the ground still entertaining Eva from costume's story about her girlfriend.

As I nod at Eva, the pad of his fingers slowly travels across the flesh of my thigh.

I stop breathing.

No one else has noticed, packed into this tight corner in the dark. Goosebumps raise where his finger traces.

I don't even have to look at him to know he's noticed the effect he has. His minute actions increase, until he's blatantly rubbing my thigh. A wave of heat floods me, pulsing with every brush of his fingers. The crowded bar, with all our colleagues surrounding us, makes my head rush. If his hand continues to move upwards, those strokes would eventually reach the place between my thighs…

"I'm getting a drink." I announce to the group standing on unstable feet, cutting off Eva.

I catch his eye as I turn for the bar, the heat in his eyes unmistakable despite the smile he's biting back. I glare and flounce to the bar, my half full wine glass still in hand.

I reach the bar and down my glass as I wait for a bartender.

Suddenly, I feel heat on my back and know he's followed me. I want to lean backwards onto his chest but I'm hyper-aware of all the eyes in this place.

Leaving the sanctuary of the group, he is much more

vulnerable to being recognized. No one has asked him for an autograph yet, thank God, but it's only a matter of time.

A tingle shoots down my spine as his hand rests on my hip, out of view of the crowds around us.

He leans closer, "Something got you worked up?"

Gulping, I look into his piercing blue eyes. "We're in public."

His eyes flutter as he bends closer to my face.

"I think that's working you up more, isn't it baby?" he whispers. "Such naughty thoughts to have out in the open."

I release my breath slowly, a blush spreading across my cheeks.

He chuckles. The bastard knows exactly what he does to me.

Turning his body inwards, pressing me against the bar and shielding me from view, he bends to my ear, his breath making me shiver. "Meet me in the bathroom."

Before I have a chance to reply, he stalks off into the crowd.

"*Pour vous?*" the bartender asks.

"*Ne t'inquiète pas.*" I mumble, glancing back at the crew. No one looks in my direction.

Placing my empty glass on the bar, I follow Danny through the crowd, anticipation tight in my belly.

As I push the bathroom door open, hands grab me and push me against the wood. My whimper of surprise muffled as his lips crash onto mine.

I attack his lips in a frenzy, the heat in my body overwhelming as I taste the tequila on his tongue.

He lodges a thigh between mine and I gasp at the pressure. My hands reach the hem of his shirt and wander up, tracing the warm skin of his toned back.

"Is this what you want, baby?" he groans, as he kisses along my jaw and down my neck. Pressing open mouths kisses along my collarbone and across my chest, he pulls my top down and takes a nipple between his teeth.

I whimper and grind down on him, my head rolling back on the door with a thump. My skirt rises up until it's resting scandalously around my hips leaving just the small material of my soaked underwear rubbing against his denim clad thigh.

I wonder if there's anyone on the other side of the door, if anyone can tell what Danny's doing to me. My heart races as I squeeze my thighs around his leg, the pressure almost making me black out.

"That's it, baby," he says, as I run my hands through his hair and tug, pulling his face back to mine.

He grabs my thigh and wraps it around his waist, his hands reaching around to clasp my ass to help grind me into him.

"I'm close," I whisper in disbelief.

He huffs a laugh, "Good girl, grind on my leg. Come with all your friends outside waiting for you."

I can't help the moan that escapes at the thought, tumbling me over the edge. He puts his lips back on mine and squeezes my thigh with his fingers as I crest the wave.

As I come down, he pecks kisses across my face. I can't catch my breath, I don't want to.

I reach for his buckle, eager for more, but he grabs my hands. "Not here. Let me take you home."

I take a calming breath and it's all I can do to nod my head. The bastard has robbed me of the ability to speak.

Furious, I grab his perfect face and press kisses to his lips, tugging again at his belt.

He laughs. "Freckles, I want to make tonight last but I won't if you keep this up."

Nodding, I raise my hands to my flushed face trying to catch my breath. "You go out first, I'll meet you outside."

He shoots me a wicked grin as he adjusts himself in his jeans.

"I'll get your stuff," he says, pressing a final kiss to my lips and reaching for the door.

"And pay your tab," I say, unable to stop my dopey grin.

He rolls his eyes and shoots me a wink as he pulls the door open.

I turn to the sink and run my hand under the cool water, futilely attempting to calm the heat burning me from the inside out. I imagine him heading back to the crew, lips swollen from my kisses, and making my excuses as he grabs my bag from my chair. I stamp down on the part of me swooning at the gesture.

Taking a steadying breath, I pull the bathroom door open and run to the exit, keeping my head down so no one notices me.

When I step outside, he's across the street looking out at the canal, my small shoulder bag clenched in his large hand. Biting down my smile, I cross to him and gently pull my bag from his clasp. He flashes me a small smile, the light of the canal reflecting in his eyes. I blink away the surge of affection at that simple gesture.

The sounds of the crowded bar drifts away as we wander up the street. I was ready to fish my phone out to order a car but I want to stay in this moment for a little bit longer.

Our fingers play together by our sides.

"You're really hot when you dance," Danny tells me, smirking.

I laugh, "Ah yes, the good old two step." I jump to the side and start swaying on my feet whilst rhythmically clicking my fingers. "How irresistible."

He chuckles, "Nah, more like when you did a bit of this." He steps closer to my body before spinning around so his back is to my front. He shakes his hips in a poor imitation of twerking and throws his arms wide.

I cackle and playfully swat his ass. "Get off, I didn't do that!"

"Oh yes you did," Danny says, throwing an arm around me, pulling me close and tucking me against his side. "It was very tasteful. I enjoyed it immensely."

I laugh again and pull back, looking up into his face, "You're just saying that because you can't dance for shit."

"Hey, I'll have you know that I have been known to throw some shapes," he says, affronted but with a laughing glint in his eye. That night in the Jazz bar proved that he definitely knows what he's doing on the dance floor.

"Throw some shapes? Are you a middle aged dad at a wedding?"

"Ha ha ha," he mocks as I choke on my own laughter. He slows and turns to me. His long fingers gently tilt my head until his lips are on mine and my laughter is swallowed on a sigh. My belly coils as he playfully bites my lip.

"Let's go home," he says quietly. I nod quickly, my body eager to be close to him.

"I need to see what kind of shapes you can make," I say cheekily and I can taste his smile on my lips.

Chapter 34

DANNY

A significant weight leaves my shoulders as soon as I am no longer contractually obligated to work for my father. My newly lightened shoulders are, however, currently weighed down by the raging hangover pounding my head.

Blinking my eyes open against the sun flooding through the window, I look over at the woman stretched out beside me. If there's one thing I've learned about Anya over the last few months is that she sleeps like the dead.

I press a kiss to her forehead to see where she's at. If she stirs immediately, I've kickstarted her waking process, if not, I'm not going to see those big hazel eyes for at least another hour. Her eyelids flicker but there's no sign of life.

Smiling, I roll onto my side and pick up my phone. Dead. I reach for the charger but remember it's buried at the bottom of my backpack.

I clamber out of bed, quietly closing the door behind me.

Yawning, I flick the kettle on before plugging my phone into Anya's charger. I chuckle at the memory of her confused face when I asked to borrow hers on the train. She's looked at me as if I had asked her to run away with me to Cambodia. On the journey back to London, I'm sure she'll be more amenable to sharing.

We haven't discussed what the next plan is, but after last night, I know what I want. I'll follow that girl anywhere, but it won't be in the dark. I want to hold her hand and touch her in public. I don't want to police the smiles she tugs at my lips or stop myself from brushing the hair out of her eyes.

My phone finally turns on with the telltale buzz of a thousand notifications. Frowning, I glance at the messages and missed calls I've received. There are dozens from Pip but mostly it's my agent, Travis.

Glancing at the time, I decide it's too late to call my sister but I care significantly less for Travis' sleep so click his name instead.

He answers on the first ring, as if he's been sat by the phone. Waiting.

"Dan, thank god. Have you spoken to anyone? The press? Production?"

My brow creases. That's definitely not how I thought this conversation would go. "What? No, I've been asleep and my phone died."

"Good man. Listen, I've been talking with Tracy over at Pepper and Whiteman and they want you to stay quiet. I've already spoken with Phillipa so she knows and if you do get caught the answer is *no comment*, understand?"

"Understand what? What the hell are you talking about, Travis?"

There's silence on the other end. "Look, all you need to know is that it's being handled and all you need to do is lay low. Stay in Paris for a few more days and order room service. But remember, *no comment*."

He hangs up.

I glance at the black screen, my confusion mixing with dread. There have been a few times in my career that Travis has guided me on what to say to the press, New Year's Eve being one of them, but it still doesn't explain what the hell is going on. I quickly scan through the messages my sister left but they're all just her asking me to call her back

It's probably time to wake her up.

The first thing I hear is her sniffles.

"What happened?" I ask sharply.

"You haven't seen?"

"Seen what?"

"The news, it's everywhere."

"What's everywhere?"

Pip cries. "Fuck, it's so–I can't even say it."

Terror grips me by the throat. "Say what, Pip, for god's sake!"

"He's not been named yet, but from the way everyone is freaking out it's pretty much confirmed." She sniffs. "It's Dad." The way she spits his name makes it clear he's not in mortal danger.

Frustrated, I pull my phone away from my ear and with shaking fingers search my father's name. Nothing comes up with his name attached but plenty of articles crop up instead.

HOLLYWOOD PRODUCER ACCUSED OF SEXUAL ASSAULT

My heart pounds in my chest. I pull my phone back to my ear but wince when I hear Pip's sobs.

"Pip, take a breath." I say, my heart thudding in my ears.

"Breathe in, and out."

She takes a shaky breath.

"I don't understand." I grip my hair in my hand. "Who's saying that this is him?"

"I don't know, but why else are we being asked to keep quiet? I'm sure you've had the no comment instruction?"

"Yeah." Dread forms like a rock in my gut. "Do we know—" I swallow barely able to stomach the words. "Do we know who?"

Pip takes a breath. "They think it's Georgia."

Georgia, the cheerful blonde the same age as Pip. Georgia who carefully highlights all my scripts and adds smiley faces to the ends of emails. My father's assistant.

I collapse onto the rickety bar stool in the kitchen. "Fuck." I swallow harshly. "Is she okay?"

"I don't know. I've been told not to contact her by the lawyers."

"There are lawyers involved?"

"Yeah," Pip says weakly.

"Have you heard from Mum?"

"Yeah," Pip scoffs. "She's checked into a facility in upstate New York, no phones but lots of Chateau Lafite probably."

"Where are you?"

"I'm at home."

"Have you slept at all?"

"No."

"Is anyone with you?"

"No," she sniffles again.

"Okay, can Cassie come and be with you?"

"She's in London doing a talk show."

I curse. "Okay, don't answer the phone, don't talk to anyone, if it's not me or Travis. Don't go online. Try to get some sleep."

"I'll try."

"I'll call you back soon."

I hang up and throw my phone onto the counter. Taking a deep breath, I brace myself and call my father. No answer. Of course. I'm glad he didn't pick up. I don't even know what I would say to him.

"Hey." I turn to see Anya leaning against the kitchen door. "What's wrong?"

The sight of her in my button down, with mussed hair and a puffy face, would normally start my heart back to beating.

Instead, I see my very disheveled *assistant*.

Horror slices through me like a knife and I clear my throat roughly. "I need to go."

Anya straightens. "Now? I thought we could spend the day together."

"I uh–I need to go back to my hotel." I brush past her, carefully angling my body away from hers.

In the bedroom, I quickly pull my jeans on, grateful when my shirt appears on the bed so I don't have to ask for it back.

"Will I see you later?" Any asks, tightening her robe and following me back to the kitchen.

"Uh—" I shove my phone in my pocket. "Yeah, sure."

I fumble to the door, my mind unable to keep up with my body.

"Uhm, okay then," Anya says, as she bites her bottom lip. I fight the urge to pull it away with my thumb and instead press a chaste kiss to her cheek. I mutter a quick goodbye before closing her door behind me.

I curse myself as soon as I land on the sunny street. I have no hat or sunglasses and no Jaques on call. The opposite of my instructions to lay low. I turn and march down the road, my footsteps heavy and strides long. I need to get away from here.

I reach the corner of the street where I once turned back and carry on. I don't look up once on the long walk back to my hotel, only noting that I've arrived when the cobblestone path turns to the marble floor of my hotel. Which is when I see Callum McBride walking towards me.

As soon as he spots me his face light up with a gleeful expression as he walks towards me.

"Well hello stranger, thought you'd be hiding out with all the gossip swirling today."

I clench my jaw and hold his gaze. "I don't know what you're talking about."

McBride chuckles. "Of course not. Say hello to Annie for me — the apple really doesn't fall far from the tree, eh?"

McBride moves to walk past me with a winning smile on his face but I step in his path.

"It's tragic," I say. "How desperate you are to get my attention. It's pathetic, honestly. I'm sorry that you feel like you can't get to where you want to be in your life without using me to do it." His bright grin dims slightly. "Have a good one."

I clap him on the shoulder before I walk away from him without looking back.

Chapter 35

ANYA

The apartment is empty without Danny in it.

It takes me less than an hour to clean the entire place, my frenzied mind making the process a blurred whirlwind.

Once I'm finished and standing in the middle of a pristine room, I check my phone to see if Danny has messaged. Nothing.

I bite my lip before pulling up his name.

Me: *Everything okay?*

Before I press send, my phone buzzes in my hand and I answer before really reading the name.

"Hi," I say with relief.

"Hi Anya, you guys get back okay last night?" Devon's cheerful voice echoes through the phone.

"Oh uhm, yeah. I got back to my apartment and Danny's at his hotel room now." There, that's definitely not a lie.

Devon chuckles. "Great, listen I've booked your train home for tomorrow lunchtime. I've sent you the details." My stomach clenches. That's it, twenty four hours left in Paris. I hear a door close on the other side of the phone and footsteps on a metal staircase. "Listen, keep this between us but I'm jumping on prep for a new film back in London. It's not confirmed and probably won't start for at least a few months, but I would want you to come with me as my production assistant."

Confusion almost knocks me over. "Me?" I ask numbly.

"Yes, I think you got a pretty short stick on this one, what with ferrying Covington around. You did an amazing job though, he's definitely been a lot easier to handle than imagined from this end. But I want to see what you can do in production. What do you say?"

My mind spins. Honestly, I woke up this morning thinking my career was over, that I was going to go public with Danny and steer clear of the industry for fears of nepotism allegations smearing my name. But now I've got a job offer that's nothing to do with him, that's purely because of the connections I've made myself.

"I'd love to," I say breathlessly.

"Lovely, well as I say it's not had the green light yet, so nothing might come from it, but I wanted to let you know I'm thinking about you. Travel safe tomorrow and enjoy some time at home. I'll email you in a few weeks with the details."

I hang up, mind reeling. A few months ago I was ready to give up this industry entirely, but now it looks like I have a chance to keep going. To figure out what's next. I always thought I'd end up the next Gwendoline Marcs, but being the next Devon might not be so bad either.

My phone still shows the unsent text to Danny. I want to tell him. I want him to be happy for me, to say I deserved it. I delete my message and start again.

Me: *When can I see you later? Got my train tickets for tomorrow.*

No text bubble appears so I angrily shove my phone in my

pocket.

I'm not moping around waiting for a man to message me. I have a new job lined up and it's my last day in Paris. I'm going out.

I swing my bag over my shoulder and take the stairs two at a time, emerging onto the street a few seconds later.

I've been in the city for nearly two months, and almost all of that time has been spent wrapped up with Danny inside these four walls. I need to explore.

I hop on the metro and emerge on the Right Bank. First stop is Musée D Orsay. I wait in a too-long line and emerge into the main hall, large vaulted ceilings allowing light to shower over the delicate sculptures. It's easy to see how the building was once a train station, the large clock face at the back of the hall looming over the tourists meandering below.

I take my time wandering in and out of every room, my shoes clipping against the hollow floor. I take photos of the famous artwork lining the walls but their beauty seems dull today. I take loops around the museum in a daze and by the time I emerge back onto the street it's past lunchtime. I check my phone. No word.

I ring my mother as I walk along the river.

"Cabbage," she greets me, finally tugging a smile to my lips.

"*Coucou mama.*"

"*C'est une vrait parisienne.*"

I laugh. "Not for much longer. I have my return ticket for tomorrow."

"I'm so excited to see you," my mother says.

I look out on the glistening Seine, the water churning past the banks where people sit with their feet dangling towards the water, sharing a bottle of wine.

"Me too."

"I'm sorry Cabbage, I have to go, my next class is starting."

We say our goodbyes with a promise to let her know when I'm on the train. I turn away from the river continuing my stroll until I end up in the Marais.

I buy a crépe from a stall but can only manage a few bites before I feel sick and throw it away.

It's only later when I sit at a cafe with the bags of gifts I've bought my mum and Rosie that I let myself think of Danny again. I don't know what sent him fleeing my apartment, what got him to clam up so much that he was almost unrecognizable from the funny, charming man I've come to know.

I glance at my phone again. Still nothing. I click into the message thread but see my message is still on read.

My blood pounds in my ears as I pull up Pip's name, but I don't know what to say. *'Hey your brother is being weird right when I think our relationship might be ending.'* Way to sound like a loser. Maybe he's just decided to end this now, before it gets complicated? Something has to have happened to trigger this, I know it. We went to sleep last night tangled in each other's arms after a night of laughter and fun. What happened between last night and this morning?

Downing my coffee and regretting the fact that it's not Irish, I gather my belongings and place my expensive sunglasses over my eyes.

At my building, I stumble up the stairs, my feet heavy from a day of walking away from my problems. I rummage in my bag for my key and finally look up. Danny's sat outside my door. As he unfurls his long legs, he leans against the door frame, as if exhaustion has taken the energy from his limbs.

I gesture for him to move aside and open the door. We say

nothing but I can't help from leaning slightly into his warmth, savoring what I already know is the last time I'll be able to do it.

I ignore him as I place my bags on the side table, fidgeting with the paper bags to avoid looking at him.

"I brought wine." Danny pulls my attention and waves the bottle in his hand. The same one we shared on the bank of the Seine.

"I'll get the glasses." There's no need to drink from the bottle now.

Chapter 36

DANNY

Sat on Anya's cream couch, I can hardly pull my eyes from her. She looks sad, resigned. I've spent my day frantically refreshing every news and social media site, so I know the news hasn't dropped yet. But she knows. She knows something has happened, something bad. I wonder if I'll ever meet another person who understands me so completely ever again.

"Are you ready?" she asks. Ready for me to tell her what has caused me to go off grid. I see her steel herself, her beautiful shoulders straightening.

"I had a call this morning from Travis." I take a sip of wine, the tender stem of the glass fragile in my hand. "There's going to be a story, and it's probably about my father."

She nods. "What kind of story?"

I wince and take another sip. The story tumbles out of me, the fragments of information I've been given.

Anya pales. "Did you know?"

I rear back in shock. It feels like she's punched me in the gut. I rest my head in my hands, the heel of my palm finding moisture on my eyelashes.

"I'm–I didn't mean." She shifts closer, her small palm resting on my back.

"It's okay," I sniff, straightening. "No. I didn't know." I release my breath slowly, hoping my anger eases from my chest. "I— I knew he would cheat on my mother. There was a cycle. He would be off on a long job and then when he'd come back there'd be a huge row and she would pack up and go on a yoga retreat or a spa trip. This time it's an upscale rehab," I scoff. "But I didn't know he would do *this*."

Anya's hand rubs my back, and I resist the urge to bend towards her like a flower searching for the warmth of the sun.

I turn to her, her brown hair tumbling past her shoulders and her eyes bright. "I think," I croak. "I think a part of me knew what kind of man he is. I mean I know what he is like with me. I just… I don't know, it feels naive to think that I didn't know when he was always–" I cut off and push my hand through my hair, tugging at the strands as if it will pull my jumbled thoughts together.

Anya moves her hand to smooth down my hair.

My jaw clenches, forcing the words out. "The fact that it's out, and everyone knows what kind of person he is and that my parent's marriage is a complete sham…" I glance at her big eyes, shining at me, and spill the words that have been burning me from the inside out. "It feels like a weight has been lifted."

"I understand," she says, her thumb resting on my tight jaw smoothing the ache.

"Isn't that awful?" I whisper.

"It's not awful." Her hand cups my jaw. "He's an abuser, he's emotionally tormented you for years. I'm sorry that he's hurt someone else, but it's not on you."

I know I shouldn't but I can't stop myself. I kiss her, the

feel of her lips under mine the only thing my mind can comprehend.

She deepens the kiss, plunging her tongue into my mouth. I grasp her thighs and tug until she's straddling me, lining us up perfectly. My hands move, cupping her securely to me as I raise to my feet and carry her to the bedroom.

I gently lay her on the bed and she brushes her cool fingers against my cheek. I capture her lips in mine, pouring all the love I haven't yet voiced into my kiss. Our hands roam, tender caresses and gentle touches. Our clothes fall to the floor and my heart feels like it's ready to burst out of my chest.

We make love and afterwards, as I cradle her in my arms and press kisses to the freckles dotting her cheeks, I pray it's not for the last time.

Chapter 37

ANYA

I wake the next morning to a faint buzzing. Blearily, I raise my head from the pillow and reach beside me, searching for a hard body that's usually curled around me.

Finding nothing but empty space and squinting against the light, I reach for my phone on the nightstand.

I have twelve missed calls. Furrowing my brow and wondering why anyone is calling me after my contract is up, I scroll to the messages and find one from Jess.

Jess: Have you seen Twitter?

With dread sinking in my stomach, I flip through the app and find the number one trending topic 'Covington'. My heart in my mouth, I quickly flick through the posts until I come across a news article.

SEXUAL ABUSE ALLEGATIONS BROUGHT AGAINST
CHARLES COVINGTON BY FORMER ASSISTANT

Scrolling, I find more and more references to the assault, including a detailed profile on Charles' former assistant, Georgia.

Then, I find something that nearly makes me drop my phone. It's a grainy picture of Danny from the other night with the caption:

PLAYBOY DANNY COVINGTON SPOTTED AT POPULAR PARIS CLUB WITH MYSTERY BRUNETTE

And there I am, wrapped around Danny as we leave the club.

There isn't just one photo. There are dozens. Him pulling me towards him for a kiss, his arm wrapped around me, then us both in peels of laughter. The only saving grace is I'm not named, and the pictures are dark enough to perhaps not identify me. But the amount of calls from the crew makes it pretty clear we've not got away with it completely.

Heart racing, I see one final post– *'Like father like son'*– before I fling my phone across the mattress and jump out of bed, buttoning Danny's discarded shirt up with shaking fingers.

Taking a breath, I open the door to find him sitting on the couch with his head in his hands, his phone resting on the table in front of him.

I cross the room to his side and run my fingers through his hair.

"Hey," I say, softly. "Are you okay?"

He laughs humorously and shakes my hand off with a shake of his head.

He sighs as he stands, clad only in black boxers.

We look at each other. My heart is racing as I desperately scan his face for any signs of panic. His bloodshot eyes can barely catch mine.

He licks his lips. "I need to go." He breezes past me on his way back to the bedroom, moving so fast I feel my hair whip in his wind stream.

"You don't have to go yet. Stay a while and take a breath."

"I don't need a breath," he says tugging on his jeans.

"Look, it will be okay, this will blow over." He remains silent as he begins to pull his shoes on. It's a repeat of yesterday, but instead of confusion my thoughts swirl with panic.

"Can I have my shirt?"

I clutch it to my chest. Somehow I know this shirt is going to be the last piece of him I'll ever get, his walls slamming down like a shutter and locking me out.

"Anya," he snaps. "My shirt."

Numbly, I unbutton the shirt and tug it off my shoulders, turning my back to him in a show of shyness I've not possessed since that first morning we woke up together. His attitude would have normally made me spit a snarky comment back at him but my voice is lost. Abandoning me alongside the comforting cotton of his button down.

Wordlessly, I hand it to him and pull on the robe hanging on the door.

"Are we not going to talk about this?"

"Talk about what?" he says flatly, pulling his jeans on.

"Don't be obtuse, Danny. It's not a good look."

He runs a frustrated hand through his hair. "I don't know what you want me to say."

"Is it–" I lick my lips, "–is it your dad or is it…us?"

His silence is all the answer I need.

"It's over, Anya," he says softly. So softly I almost don't hear him.

"What?" I whisper.

He finally catches my eye. "It's over." The words roar in my ears.

"Are you joking?" I choke, following him as he rushes through the apartment.

No response. "That's it? A few photos and you end this just like that?"

"It's not just the photos," he snaps, refusing to look at me.

"Then I don't see what the issue is, why are you doing this?"

"This is serious, Anya!" he explodes, his hand running through his hair. "Those pictures are not going to go away. With all the stuff that's come out about my *father*–" Danny spits the word with disgust. "This will only get worse, and the worse it gets for the family, the worse it gets for us. Anya, they're not going to leave us alone, especially now. It's a bloody miracle the press haven't figured out it's you yet, but it's only a matter of time. And then think what they'll say."

Understanding dawns slowly. They'll say he was taking advantage of his assistant. Just like his father.

"Danny, you can't think like that. You're nothing like *him*."

"They don't know that," he cries. "To the world I'm a washed-up child actor who is sailing on the wings of a predator and snorting lines of coke on the weekends."

Helplessly, I reach for him. "But you know that's not you."

"But they think that, Anya! They do, and there is nothing we can do about it…"

How can we go from the other night to this? Just days ago I had had to bite my lip to keep the words on my tongue. The words that I've felt for so long, but been too scared to say out loud. My mind whirls as I try to come up with another solution, a way to stop this from happening. But he beats me to it.

"Look, it's been fun, but let's not kid ourselves anymore than we already have. There's no need to make this anything more than it was, Anya. I can't do you any favors, so we might as well just end it here."

I see red. "Favors? Don't do that. Don't make this out to be something it wasn't just so you can do this to me. You know we're not like that, that we never have been. You're the one who reassured *me* when I was having doubts. We both knew how damaging this could be to my reputation but we did it anyway. If this gets out no one will touch me with a ten foot pole. I'll just be the girl that slept with the lead actor." Numbly, I realize I haven't even told him about the new job with Devon.

"Then where can we go from here?" he asks, exhausted.

He doesn't want it out because it'll look like he's taking advantage, me for the same reasons.

Our relationship can't survive in the shadows forever, we both knew that going in. It's what we agreed and what we felt coming even as we fooled ourselves it wouldn't matter.

We stare at each other, and I try to drink him in, commit his face to memory. I know by the way his eyes rove my face that he is doing the same. He nods finally and turns on his heel.

"This was never going to end any other way, was it?" I call from behind, the wobble in my voice killing me.

He stops, unable to look at me. "No, it wasn't," he says before pulling the door open and slamming it behind him.

The silence of the empty apartment swallows me whole. I take in the room. I know I will never be able to be here and not picture him sitting at the window with the guitar that will always be his, or emerging from the kitchen with a cup of coffee, or slamming the door behind himself as he walks out of my life. Forever.

Chapter 38

DANNY

Getting off the flight at LAX forces me to walk through a parade of paparazzi. My hat and glasses do little to prevent people calling to me. I can usually ignore the voices but I can't help my ears tuning in, searching for Anya's name.

"Danny, anything to say about your father?"

"Danny, have you spoken to your father?"

"Danny, where's your sister?"

"Danny, who's the girl?"

I tell myself that if they didn't have Anya's name yet, I broke things off at the right time. I have to hope that the crew won't out her either. Everyone on set liked her, no one would willingly throw her under the bus like this. Hopefully.

I was a fool to think that I could have anything good, that I could meet a normal girl and have a normal relationship. We couldn't even go out in public once without it falling into the hands of anyone with a camera phone.

A car service picks me up and drives me to Pip's house. I have my own key so let myself in.

"Pip?" I call, dropping my bag at my feet.

"Danny?" she calls from upstairs, and she descends in a

239

baggy sweatshirt and leggings, her usually styled hair pulled into a messy bun. She envelops me in a hug and I lean on her a little too much. Our whole childhood, we have never had a relationship like we've had the last few years. Now it's us against the world. Literally.

Pip pulls away and looks behind me. "Where's Anya?"

I clear my throat. "Paris."

Pip blinks. "I thought she would have come with you."

I ignore her and walk to the kitchen.

"Danny," Pip says, disappointingly.

"Did you see it?"

"See what?"

"What people are saying about her."

"About who? Anya? What are people saying?"

"Nothing," I'm forced to admit. "Yet. But it's only a matter of time."

Pip's eyes narrow. "So you broke up with her?"

"It was always going to end this way." I wonder if I keep saying it, it will eventually hurt less.

"You're an idiot."

"Excuse me?"

"You pushed her away *now*, when you need her the most?"

"Yes, I pushed her away now," I snap. "Our family is in the middle of a huge scandal because our father couldn't stop taking advantage of his employees." I make an angry gesture at myself. Can't she see what I can?

Pip gasps. "Danny, you can't seriously think that there is any similarity between what he" –she stumbles over the words– "has done and your relationship with Anya."

"Of course I do!" The anger inside me bursting out. "Everyone will think that."

"Let them think it! As long as you and the people who love you know the truth, it doesn't matter."

I raise my hands, "I can't listen to this. It's not enough."

"You love her Danny, of course it's enough."

I freeze and stare at her.

"You love her, don't you?"

Words stick in my throat. The air in the room evaporates.

"I'm tired," I manage to grit out. "I'm going to bed."

I let my bag drop to the floor in the bedroom Pip keeps for me in the house. I don't bother to open the blinds or turn on the light before collapsing onto the plush bedding.

Pip hired an interior designer to craft every inch of her house, including my room. Mahogany furniture with soft white furnishings give the room a cozy feel, but I can't get comfortable. The bed is too soft, the duvet too silky, the room too quiet. I close my eyes and picture Anya's bedroom, noises from the bustling street below filtering through the Juliet balcony, her warm body curled around mine and her hair tickling my nose.

You love her, don't you?

The question spins in my head.

Falling in love with Anya was easier than falling asleep. Falling out of love with Anya will be the hardest thing I'll ever have to do.

Chapter 39

ANYA

It's very easy to feel like the last few months have been a complete dream when I'm back on Rosie's couch drinking cheap Sauvignon Blanc and sobbing.

I got back to London yesterday, the seat next to me empty of any grumpy, attractive men. I did manage to make it all the way back to Rosie's place before completely breaking down, where I quickly realized that not telling my best friend anything about the man I have been secretly in love with for the past two months was probably not my best idea.

"Danny Covington." Rosie repeats for the fifth time after I've spilled the whole story to her.

"Yes," I wail, blowing my nose.

"Danny Covington." It's like she's having a software malfunction.

"Rosie," I moan, gulping my non-French wine like it's water.

"Danny Cov—"

I throw a cushion at her, her hands catch it before it dislodges the glasses perched on her nose.

"I'm sorry! It's just taking me a second to absorb. Why didn't you tell me?"

I sniff. "We didn't tell anyone."

"Does your mum know?"

"No. Only Jaques the driver. And his sister." I wince. "And Cassie."

"His sister? Wait, Cassie as in *Cassandra?*" Rosie shrieks.

I nod miserably.

"Oh my god. This is the best day ever."

I shoot her a flat look. "I mean, you poor thing." Rosie moves to my side and wraps her arm around me.

"I feel like such an idiot."

"You're not an idiot, he's an idiot." She rubs her hand along my arm. "If anything, it sounds like he was trying to do the right thing."

I side eye her.

"Hey, I don't know the guy, because *someone* didn't introduce me, but from what you've said it sounds like he has a lot going on and he wanted to protect you from it."

I break out in fresh sobs.

Rosie huffs and rests her head on mine. "Here," she says, handing me back my wine glass. "Let's get really drunk, watch *Better You Know* and throw chocolates at the TV Legally Blonde style."

I take what I hope it a calming breath. "I'd like to do one of those things."

"Throw chocolate at the TV? Me too, I love doing that."

I laugh weakly and allow Rosie to fill my glass.

* * *

A few days of moping on Rosie's couch and my mum calls me

home with the promise of her famous onion soup and a hug.

As soon as I arrive through the front door, I'm swept into her arms and I lean on her a bit too heavily. I haven't told her anything about Danny but I'm sure she's figured out there's something up. This is not the welcome home she was expecting to have to give.

"Come sit, I already made your soup."

She scoops the soup into two bowls, the ceramic chipped and faded from years of use.

"Thank you," I say, trying to keep the tears from falling.

I've never had a break up hurt this much before. Especially the end of a relationship that I walked into with open eyes. But I refuse to let the burning behind my eyes turn to tears. I cried enough huddled on Rosie's shoulder to have anything left to give.

"Do you like it?" Mum asks before I've taken a bite. I roll my eyes and make a show of the first sip, groaning with delight.

"Delicious," I tell her.

"Now, tell me all about it," she says, taking her own spoon in hand.

I nod and take another sip to stall. "Yeah it was great, it's going to be a good film when it's out." She's still looking at me expectantly. "My job wasn't exactly in the thick of it, but I've made some good connections." She blinks at me. "And I might have my next thing lined up so that's good." I trail off lamely.

Mum nods. "And what about the man?"

"What man?" I shift in my seat.

"Anya," She sends me a knowing look.

I gnaw on my lip. "What about him?" I ask hoarsely.

"What happened?"

"What happened with what?"

"With that Danny Covington boy." How the hell did she even know? "I may be your mother but I'm not blind, I saw the pictures."

"Nothing happened, okay!" I burst out. "It wasn't ever going to be a long term thing, so let's just drop it. No one even knows that was me."

Mum holds her hands up placatingly. "Okay, okay." She goes back to her soup. "Why wasn't it going to be long term?"

I drop my spoon in my bowl with a clatter. "Because I'm me and he's *him*."

"What's that supposed to mean? Did he tell you he was better than you?"

"No, no, it's just…we're very different people and we want different things."

"What different things?"

"He wants to do music and I want my career."

Mum nods as if she's following along. "So you both want jobs?"

"Yes."

"Well cabbage, lots of couples have jobs. I don't understand what the problem is."

I squirm in my seat. "It would look bad."

"Why would it look bad?"

"Because it would look like I used him to get ahead in my career and he would look like he took advantage of me."

She looks at me shocked. "Did he take advantage of you?"

"No! Of course not. But that's what people would say."

"Anya," Mum sighs. "Since when have you cared about what other people say? It seems to me that if you have each other it shouldn't matter what anyone says about you and your relationship."

"Yeah, well," I shrug, my soup going blurry. "Well, it's done now, so…" I trail off, clutching my spoon tightly between my fingers.

Mum rubs my shoulder comfortingly. "Oh, cabbage. Right, tell me more about this new job."

Chapter 40

DANNY

Pip decided that it would be helpful to have the entertainment news on 24/7. I think it's akin to torture.

Trevor and our lawyers have been trying to get in touch. I should turn my phone off but I keep it on, in the futile wish that Anya will call. Instead, I meticulously scroll. The official channels will report on updates regarding *him* so instead I'm desperately searching for her name.

Dread has been a constant companion in my chest ever since those first pictures came out. That dread has increasingly spread, tightening around my throat like a snake cutting off air. It's not eased even though I haven't found any evidence anyone has linked Anya to me. It grows and grows each time I don't find anything. If no one knows about her, did I even have to lose her in the first place?

A knock sounds at the front door. Only people with the access code to the front gate would be able to get this far. I peek out the window.

My jaw clenches and blood rushes to my ears. The knocking resumes.

"Will you open the goddamn door?" My father booms.

Thankful Pip is in the shower on the other side of the house, I swing the door open. I stand like granite, resting my hand on the door frame.

"Finally," Charles huffs, attempting to walk past me. My arm strains with how tight I'm clutching the frame, blocking him from entering. Fortunately I've been making the most of Pip's home gym since I arrived.

"What are you doing here?" My jaw hurts from how tightly it's clenched.

Redness creeps up his cheeks. "I'm here to see my children." His chest puffs out as if he said a proud statement. He's never been proud to be my father before.

"The people in this house don't have fathers."

I expect him to go for the arm extended in front of his purpling face, so I don't expect him to put his weight against the door. The door bounces against the wall. I step in front of him.

"Don't tell me you believe the bullshit that's being spread about me."

"You're saying it's not true?" Maybe when I first heard the news, I needed to know whether it was real or not. Whether I could believe that my father would be capable of something like this. But now, I don't even need to ask. I know it's true. I know the man in front of me like a nightmare I can't forget. There is no doubt in my mind he's the monster everyone says he is. He's been that same monster for my entire life.

"Of course it's not true. She has some real problems, that one, I tell you. I just wanted to help her, give her some friendly career advice. The whole thing has been blown well out of proportion."

My fingers curl in my hand, disgusted at the filth pouring

out of his mouth.

"I need you to leave."

"Last I checked, this was my daughter's house, not yours."

"She doesn't want you here. I don't want you here."

"You are so ungrateful, Daniel. It's not like you haven't done exactly what I have. Your pretty little assistant will turn around one day and do the exact same thing to you."

My blood turns to ice in my veins. The paralyzing fear that made me walk out of Anya's life. That I would be just like my father…

I pursued her, once I'd been with her once, I didn't give up. Was I too pushy? Did I come on too strong?

I remember the way she laughed at me on our first date, the way she would run her fingers through my hair and stand up for me even when there would be consequences for her, the way she would stress clean like she was covering up a crime scene and force her aunt's guitar into my arms. I felt her love in every action. I didn't even need the words. I didn't need her to tell me that what we had was real. I felt it every day.

I raise my head to look down into my fathers eyes. His face is blotchy with anger and his suit jacket rumpled.

"I'm not anything like you." My words don't wobble. They don't waver. With each word I aim at the man that has controlled me for my entire life, I feel myself grow taller. "I never have been and I never will. I will never threaten. I will never be cruel. I will never be anything like you. I'm ashamed to call you my father. And I never will again."

His eyes twitch and he sucks in a deep breath. Before he can say a final word I usher him backwards until he has no choice left to stand on the front door step, the LA sun streaming through the doorway, bathing him in shadow and me in warmth.

"Who do you think you are?" he splutters, "I can ruin you."

I laugh. "There's nothing you could do to me that is worse than what you've done to yourself. Have a nice life. Whatever's left of it."

I close the door in his face. It crosses my mind to collapse against the wood but I don't need the support. My own two feet have got me.

I brush my hand across my face and choke on a laugh. I want to tell Anya. I want to tell her that I stood up to him, that I cut him out of my life. For good.

But I've already cut her out too.

Chapter 41

DANNY

It's been a week since I left Anya behind and I still wake up expecting her to be there. It takes a second each morning for reality to sink in and for me to remember what happened, what I did. All my stuff has remained in my suitcase, as if my stay here is a temporary break from my real life back in Europe.

Today, I finally run out of boxers and rummage through my chaotic suitcase. My fingers brush against the little blue notebook. I sit on the bed and let the paper flick between fragments of songs and half finished thoughts.

It's almost obvious when I started falling for Anya, the lyrics transforming from angry, harsh words to soliloquies formed with love. I never told her, but I felt it, showed it in the words I scrawled across the page whilst she slept against my chest or pottered around my trailer.

The front door opening downstairs disturbs me from my memories. I stand and finish getting dressed, shoving the notebook in my pocket.

Downstairs, Cassie leans against the kitchen counter with

Pip.

"Hey," I say, reaching for a hug. "What are you doing here?"

"Came to check on you guys. How you doing?"

I glance at Pip. We've spent all our time inside, barely even stepping outside for fear of a camera or drone getting any footage.

"Getting there," I say.

Pip hands her a cup of coffee. "Well, I also came for a favor," Cassie says with a small smile.

I step to the coffee machine and place a mug under the spout. It's only when I turn around that I realize Cassie has her sights set on me. "From me?"

She takes a sip. "That song we worked on in Paris, I wondered if you would be interested in helping me finish it."

"In what way?"

"Everything, lyrics, melody, vocals."

"*My* vocals?" I ask.

"Yeah, you have an amazing voice and you worked so hard on it, I can't imagine anyone else doing it."

I sip my coffee, taking a moment to gather myself. I think of Anya's encouraging smile that night I played for her, I think of the blue book burning a hole in my pocket. "I'm in," I tell Cassie. "As long as you can help me with something."

Chapter 42

My phone rings with a call from Devon whilst I'm walking out of the local supermarket. I'm reading the label on the vitamins my mother has sworn will *'give me my energy back'*. I tried to tell her that my lack of energy is probably little to do with a Vitamin B deficiency and more likely because I can't bear to do anything apart from sit at home moping.

I throw the vitamin box back in my bag and answer as I step outside into the mild air.

"Hello?"

"Hey Anya, how have you been?"

I nod as if she can see me. "Great, thanks." I try to enthuse my voice with as much pep as I can. "You?"

"Good, good. So that job is looking to start moving in the next week. Are you okay to start on Monday?"

Monday? My stomach flips. I'm excited for a new job of course, but the prospect of walking onto a set without Danny Covington is almost too much to bear.

Pull yourself together, Anya. He's gone and he's not coming back, I straighten my shoulders.

"Monday works perfectly."

Devon rattles off an address in London and I mentally write down everything I need to do on my walk back to the car. First I need to find somewhere to live. There's no way I can commute from home or bunk on Rosie's couch for the next three months. It will be good for me, to have my own space. To put my stamp on a place that doesn't have my baby pictures hung on the walls or a spot in the corner for a guitar stand. It's what I need. Even if it makes my heart heavier in my chest.

In the quiet of my car, I take a deep breath before starting the engine. The radio clicks on as I pull onto the road. The sun is setting on the horizon and I drive towards it, squinting into the light. I can't concentrate on my driving whilst the radio hosts banter so I reach to turn it off.

"...and now a new one from Cassandra. The mystery of who's the feature on this one has gone viral. Let's see if we can figure out who he is. This is *Wish I Could*."

My whole body freezes as the song that was first played in my little Paris apartment echoes through the speakers. It's an effort to keep the car moving and my hands on the wheel as I feel my heart pounding in my chest. I find myself leaning towards the speaker, desperate to hear what I somehow know is coming.

Danny's voice fills the car. He sounds the exact same as the first time he sang for me. My stomach swoops as his smooth voice washes over me. The original version focused on Cassandra's yearning to live her life on her own terms. Now, Danny's verse laments a lost love that he wishes he could save. It's only when the song ends that I realize the wetness on my face is from my tears.

My vision blurs as I pull to a stop outside my childhood home, pulling the key out of the ignition before burying my head in my hands and letting the sobs free. This is ridiculous, how many more tears am I to shed over a *man?*

The car door opens, and my sob is replaced with a scream. I flinch back in my seat with my hand over my racing heart, but it's not a murderer standing with his hands braced against the car.

It's Danny.

I gape at him, my eyes darting from him to the radio that just played his voice. Maybe I crashed the car on the way here and here is the grim reaper preparing to move me on.

"Why are you crying?" Danny asks, the car light bathing his smooth skin in a golden ray.

"What the fuck?" is all I can say. I reach behind me with shaky hands and unbuckle the seat belt tugged painfully against my torso.

I don't even think as I take his offered hand, wincing at the sparks that travel up my arm as soon as we touch.

He lets go of me as soon as I'm upright, taking a step back. I miss his touch immediately and wrap my arms around my stomach.

"What the fuck?" I whisper again, mostly to myself.

Danny runs his hand through his hair. "Uh, hello."

"Hello?" I ask incredulously. *"Hello?"*

I press the heel of my palms to my eyes, as if I can rub away the vision of the love of my life standing before me.

"What are you doing here?" Tingles dance at the edges of my vision, but he is very much still standing in my mother's driveway.

"I..." He stops and takes a breath. "I needed to see you."

I stare at him. He walked away from me without a second glance, implying that I was taking advantage of him, that we were never going anywhere, and now he needs to *see* me?

"Why?"

He flinches and takes another deep breath. "I knew as soon as I left that I was making the worst decision of my life. I thought it was for the best. If I left like that, if you hated me and we cut it off then, I thought we would both be able to move on. But it was like cutting off my right arm. I didn't feel whole anymore, like some vital piece of me was still with you even though I was thousands of miles away.

Every time an article or a post came out about me and the mysterious girl I was seen with, or about my dad, I told myself that it was right. That it was right to leave you behind even when my body was screaming at me to pick up the phone and call you. I couldn't sleep, I couldn't think straight, I couldn't listen to music without thinking of you.

Cassie came by and asked if I would help with her album, work on that song that I only ever decided to play because you inspired me to. So I agreed. We stayed up all night and she'd fall asleep in the studio but I stayed awake until my fingers were numb. I poured everything I felt about my father, about my life, about *you* out, until I blinked one day and had an album in front of me. I finished it and I thought I would be happy, I thought it would fill me with purpose, with –I don't know–joy? But it was empty, it was empty without you. *My life* was empty without you."

He takes a deep breath, "I could have all the dreams I could ever want, but it would mean nothing without you. I love you, Anya."

His declaration spills across the quiet driveway of my childhood home. He breathes heavily as if he's just finished a marathon.

I blink at him. "I got a job."

His jaw drops slightly before he barks a laugh and rubs his hand over his face. "I spill my heart out in front of you and that's the first thing you say?"

I want to step closer but my feet feel frozen to the ground. "I got a job. I was so scared that you would end up steamrolling my career, that I would never be able to make it on my own, that I couldn't have both. A career I was proud of and—" *You.* I bite my lip before that last omission tumbles out.

"That's amazing, freckles." A bright smile tugs at his beautiful lips. "I'm so proud of you."

I brush past him, his chest brushing my shoulder. I grab my shopping out of the rear door. I don't need to see him to feel his presence lingering behind me.

"Do you like French onion soup?" I ask, turning to face him.

He blinks. "Uh, yeah?"

"Okay." I hand him the bag and turn towards the front door.

Chapter 43

DANNY

Anya's childhood home is very different to mine. Mine was a mansion in Beverly Hills and a townhouse in West London. Cold and empty and lonely. Anya's is a terraced house on a quiet street, coats piled on the banister and photos hanging on the walls. Anya barely acknowledges me as she toes her shoes off and leaves them in a neat pile by the door. I follow her lead and leave my sneakers next to hers. It feels domestic and I can't stop the hope that rises in my chest. Has she forgiven me?

She wanders down the hallway and I follow, still dutifully holding the bag she handed me. My gaze snags on the pictures on the wall. I recognize small Anya immediately, her big hazel eyes and smattering of freckles hidden behind a goofy looking full fringe.

Anya pushes open the door at the end of the hallway, the scent of onions filling the small space.

"There you are. Can you butter the bread, petit chou?" Anya's mum has her back to us, stirring a pot on the stove.

Anya glances at me out of the corner of her eye, her pretty cheeks turning pink. I can't help the grin that pulls at my mouth.

"Uh," Anya clears her throat. "So Danny's here?"

Her mum whirls around, wooden spoon in hand. "Oh!"

She pierces me with an assessing glare. I change the bag to my left hand and extend my right for her to shake. "It's lovely to finally meet you, I've heard so much about you."

Sabine shakes herself and rushes forward, ignoring my hand and pulling me into an awkward hug. Anya gently pulls the shopping from my hand, freeing my arms up to return Sabine's embrace. The top of her curly hair barely reaches my shoulder but I feel strangely comfortable.

She releases me and steps back. "It's lovely to meet you." She beams at me, her smile so similar to Anya's. "Sit, sit." She bustles me into a chair.

"Anya, get the wine." She commands her daughter without taking her eyes off me. "The nice one."

Anya rolls her eyes at me and pulls a bottle out of the rickety wine rack near the fridge.

"So Danny, what are you doing here?" I pull my eyes away from Anya as she opens the bottle with a corkscrew.

I clear my throat and look directly in her mother's eyes. "I came to ask Anya to give me another chance."

The bottle in Anya's hand pops like punctuation. She gapes at me. If she was expecting me to be more coy around her mother, she must think I'm a fool.

"Oh! Well that's just lovely." Sabine shoots her daughter a knowing grin.

Anya pours us all a glass and sits down next to me at the kitchen table. She gulps her wine quickly. She's close enough that I can brush her thigh with my knee.

Sabine peppers me with questions as she dishes up and

doesn't let up until our bowls are clean and the wine is half empty. Anya's long fingers play with the stem of the glass and it takes all my willpower not to take her hands in mine.

I chance a glance at her and see she's already looking at me.

She clears her throat. "Devon offered me that job, mum. I start on Monday."

"Oh!" Sabine exclaims and I wonder if it's a word she says often or if we're just continuously overwhelming her. "Cabbage, that's amazing. Isn't that amazing, Danny?"

The smile that overtakes my face is effortless. "It is." I can't help but feel this is a good sign, one of the obstacles we faced at the beginning that's now resolved. Anya could still turn me down but at least she'll know that she can make her own way regardless.

"I told her, I said it wouldn't matter either way for you to be together and her to work in the industry. Who cares, that's what I say!"

"Mum," Anya hisses.

"She's always wanted to work in film. She used to get the old camcorder and make home movies. Starring herself of course, I still have them all on the old computer. I'll show you—"

Anya pushes to her feet before her mother can. "I'm going to show Danny my room."

Sabine settles and raises her hands. "Of course, of course. Ignore me."

Anya nudges my shoulder until I'm out of my seat and following her up the narrow stairs. The small hallway has three doors, one propped open to reveal a family bathroom. She leads me to the first door.

Anya's room is lived in. A faded desk chair sits up against a small desk, her bed is pushed to one wall and twinkling lights stream from corner to corner. I put my hands in my pockets as she collapses against the bed. I don't want to assume and sit next to her, so instead, I wander the small space. Jewelry hangs on a small tree on her dresser and little bottles of her skin care that used to be in Chez Claudette are lined up neatly on her bedside table.

"I love your house," I say, gently flopping in the desk chair.

She waves a hand. "It is what it is."

I roll the chair towards her, getting caught on the pink rug poking underneath her bed. Eventually I'm close enough that our knees are touching. She doesn't move. I lean forward, hands dangling between my thighs,

"What are you thinking, freckles?" I ask softly.

She takes a deep breath and the hands that were neatly folded in her lap edge towards mine.

"I didn't expect this. For you to show up *here*. How did you even find this address?"

I wince. "Not my finest moment. I told Devon I wanted to send you a thank you gift."

She huffs a laugh and bites her bottom lip. I want to tug it free with my thumb but resist.

"I love you, freckles," I say again. I will say it every day for the rest of my life if she'll let me.

Anya's fingers hook around mine. I hold my breath as she twines our fingers together. "How do I know you won't just leave me again?"

I nod. "I know, I messed up. I made the biggest mistake of my life. I'm so sorry Anya. I promise I won't ever do it again."

My thumb rubs against her knuckles, soaking her in. If this is the last time I get to touch her I want to be able to remember this feeling.

"Even if—" I take a deep breath. "Even if this is too much, and we can't find a way to do this, you must know being with you has been the best time of my life."

Her tongue peeks out and wets her lips. "You have to promise to let me in. No storming off when things get complicated, we have to talk through it."

I nod, barely able to comprehend her words.

"And I'll be working this new job in London, but I don't want to be a secret anymore. If we're doing this we're done keeping it just us. I don't want to have to hide you."

"I don't want to hide you either. I'll hire some billboards and put your face on them so everyone can know."

She laughs, the sound piercing my heart and causing it to beat again. "Well, maybe we don't need to go that far."

I place my hands on her thigh. "I'll never keep us a secret again, I promise."

She raises her hands and runs her fingers through my hair. It takes everything in me not to rub into her palm like a cat.

"I love you too, Danny. I have since you gave me your shoe to open a corked bottle of wine."

I rest my forehead on hers. "Say it again?"

"I love you."

My mouth crashes onto hers, tugging her to me until she's crowded on my lap and where she belongs. Finally.

Epilogue

ANYA

I've never been VIP at a concert before but I will say it's pretty cool. There's no one crushing you from either side and the floor isn't sticky. Heaven.

Rosie is jumping up and down like a madwoman, in between pinching my arm every time a famous face reaches for the champagne in the bucket beside her. She stares at me wide eyed after Jackson Harper winks at her from across the section. I laugh and tell her with my eyes that we can freak out in the bathroom later.

Danny's arm comes around my waist as he hands Rosie and I our drinks. I reach up and kiss him. It's so freeing to be able to do that whenever I want. After much deliberation in the group chat I started with Rosie, Pip and Cassie, we soft launched our relationship to the public with a picture I took at Claudette's apartment. It was a story for a few days, before everyone moved on to something else.

The film in London wrapped up a few weeks ago, but I've already got a job lined up in LA to start in a few months. I'm nervous to make the move to the US, but Pip and Cassie have promised to hang out with me and Rosie and my mother are already planning a trip to visit. And of course, Danny will be there. He's been stuck in the recording studio in LA for almost the entire time I've been filming in London, so the chance to share a space with him again is one I do not want to give up. It's still a secret that he's making the move to music, with only our closest friends knowing, but I can't wait for the day he makes that final leap.

I lean back into Danny's embrace, trying to ignore the phone cameras I can see pointing in our direction. The public curiosity into our relationship is something that I'm still trying to get used to, but I know now what it's like to not be with him. A few candid pictures are worth it for moments like these.

I let my head fall against his firm chest, looping my hands around the arms he wraps around me. He holds me for a few minutes, swaying with me to the music before he kisses my cheek and says, "I'll be back."

I nod and let him go, turning back to Pip and Rosie as we sing along to the song.

This is my first time attending a Cassandra concert on this tour. Danny and I decided Paris would be the best show for us to see, for obvious reasons.

"Thank you Paris!" Cassie shouts from the stage. We all cheer, Pip managing to hit a pitch I didn't think was humanly possible.

"Now I have a special treat for you guys." Cassie says in between the roar of the crowd. "I don't usually play this song because I can never do it justice. This last album wasn't the easiest to write, until I was in this city."

The cheers are deafening but I almost can't hear them over the pounding in my ears. "I had no idea a friend of mine had it in him, but he picked up a guitar and helped me write what has now become my favorite song I've ever written."

I can feel the tension rising in the arena. I blindly reach out and grab Pip's hand, unbelieving. I want to scan behind me to see if Danny is coming back to me but my eyes are glued to the stage.

"So guys, give it up for *Danny Covington.*"

There's a second where my heart stops before the roar of the crowd deafens me. I scream so loud my throat gets hoarse as the love of my life steps onto the stage, a guitar looped across his chest.

He waves to the crowd and hugs Cassie. He steps up to the mic and lets the crowd lose their minds for a few seconds longer. When they die down, he says, "Thank you, this is pretty crazy."

Tears stream down my cheeks.

"I just want to say, I wouldn't be here right now if it wasn't for this city and the girl that I met here. So this is for you."

I can hardly see through my tears as he starts playing the song. Pip and Rosie put their arms around me as we sway to the music.

I guess that's the last secret we'll have to keep for a while.

Thank you for reading

I hope you enjoyed Danny and Anya's book!

If you liked this book please consider leaving a review, I'd love to hear from you!

Francesca x

Also by Francesca Shaw

The It Girls
Keep It
Book 2 (Coming Soon!)

Acknowledgments

First of all, thank YOU for giving *Keep It* a chance! It took many years for me to even admit that I'd been secretly writing a book, and nearly two years after that to get to this point. I told myself that if I can get 10 people to read this book and get some sort of enjoyment out of it I'll be happy…so fingers crossed!

Aimee, I honestly don't even know where to begin. I wouldn't be here today without your constant encouragement even when I was riddled with self doubt. You have loved this book and these characters even when I couldn't. I know I joke that you are the other half of my brain but it's completely true and I'll never be able to express my gratitude enough.

Gee, you were the first person I had ever met who had written a book! You inspired me then and you inspire me now. I hope you enjoyed being back in Paris for a little bit (and thank you for pointing out every time I overused a comma…whoops!).

Mel, thank you so much for this beautiful cover, I am so beyond thrilled with how it turned out.

Mum, thank you for not being surprised when I told you I was writing a book and for supporting me the whole time. I love you to the moon and back. And yes, I will be providing you with a censored copy.

Joey, thank you for always supporting me. Thank you for being you. I love you.

About the Author

Francesca Shaw is a twenty-something author living in London with her partner. When she's not writing romance novels, she's juggling a full time career in the film industry and reading every romance book she can get her hands on. She also lived in Paris for six months and will not shut up about it.

Follow her on Instagram and TikTok @authorfrancescashaw

You can connect with me on:
- https://www.instagram.com/authorfrancescashaw
- https://www.tiktok.com/@authorfrancescashaw